CW00410024

Life in the
Georgian Court

*For Granddad Steve, who taught me how to tell stories
and to <u>never</u> spare the gory details.*

Life in the
Georgian Court

Catherine Curzon

PEN & SWORD HISTORY

First published in Great Britain in 2016 by
Pen & Sword History
an imprint of
Pen & Sword Books Ltd
47 Church Street
Barnsley
South Yorkshire
S70 2AS

ISBN 978 1 47384 551 0

Typeset in Ehrhardt by
Mac Style Ltd, Bridlington, East Yorkshire
Printed and bound in the UK by CPI Group (UK) Ltd,
Croydon, CRO 4YY

Pen & Sword Books Ltd incorporates the imprints of Pen & Sword
Archaeology, Atlas, Aviation, Battleground, Discovery, Family
History, History, Maritime, Military, Naval, Politics, Railways, Select,
Transport, True Crime, and Fiction, Frontline Books, Leo Cooper,
Praetorian Press, Seaforth Publishing and Wharncliffe.

For a complete list of Pen & Sword titles please contact
PEN & SWORD BOOKS LIMITED
47 Church Street, Barnsley, South Yorkshire, S70 2AS, England
E-mail: enquiries@pen-and-sword.co.uk
Website: www.pen-and-sword.co.uk

Contents

Acknowledgements

This book is the culmination of a long-held dream and, without the wand waving of Kate Bohdanowicz and the Pen and Sword Books team, it might never have happened at all. Thanks are also due to the Wellcome Collection and the British Library for their wonderfully efficient and approachable staff; without them, this would be a considerably less well-illustrated volume.

The generosity and companionship of the team at T&Cake, the finest café this side of the eighteenth century, cannot be underestimated either; this book owes a lot of its existence to a particularly comfy armchair and their uniquely wonderful tea. My gratitude goes out to those who made this dream a reality by visiting my website and urging me along the road when I couldn't see for crowns and sceptres. To friends both absent and near and to Willow Winsham, thank you all for magic, mayhem and laughter.

Top billing must be reserved for Rick, my very own rakish Colonial, and our pets, especially Pippa, my constant companion and erstwhile editor.

All images are reproduced according to the credits.

All newspaper clippings, unless otherwise noted, are reproduced courtesy of the British Library Board.

Illustrations

1. Queen Anne. 1730, John Closterman, after John Faber.*
2. Sophia Electress of Hanover, mother of King George I. 1690, RB Peake.*
3. King George I. 1722, John Faber, after D Stevens.**
4. George Augustus Prince of Wales, later George II. 1724, Godfrey Kneller.*
5. King George II and Queen Caroline with their ten children. Anonymous.*
6. Queen Caroline [of Ansbach] and George Prince of Wales. 1765, Robert Pile, after Richard Houston.*
7. Frederick, Prince of Wales. 1740, C Boit, after Jacobus Houbraken.*
8. King George III. 1804, William Beechey.*
9. Queen Charlotte. 1777, Benjamin West.**
10. Princess Amelia. Arthur Mee, after JS Agar.*
11. George III and his family. 1771, Richard Earlom, after Johann Zoffany.***
12. King George III of the United Kingdom. W Lowry.*
13. Charlotte, Her Royal Highness the Princess Royal. 1801, Peltro W Tomkins.**
14. King George IV. 1827, Robert Bowyer, after John Bromley.*
15. Mrs Fitzherbert. 1792, after Richard Cosway.**
16. Her Most Gracious Majesty Caroline [of Brunswick], Queen of England. 1810, T Wageman, after Thomas A Woolnoth.*
17. The maid bringing in the breakfast finds the Prince of Wales and Mrs Fitzherbert in a dishevelled state on the morning after their marriage. 1788, James Gillray.*
18. A man disappearing into a cracked chamber pot which has the legs of woman; implying the illicit relationship between the Duke of Clarence and Mrs. Jordan. 1791, James Gillray.*

Timeline of Major Events

This timeline also incorporates (in italics) dates for the events featured in this book.

1660   *George I born*
1682   *George I and Sophia Dorothea of Celle married*
1683   *George II born*
1694   *George I and Sophia Dorothea of Celle marriage dissolved*
1701   The Act of Settlement
1705   *George II and Caroline of Ansbach married*
1709   *Anne, Princess Royal, born*
1712   *Frederick the Great born*
1714   *Queen Anne dies*
1714   *Reign of George I begins*
1715   First Jacobite rising
1715   *Louis XIV dies*
1717   *Prince George William born*
1718   *Prince George William dies*
1718   British convicts start being transported to penal colonies overseas
1718   War of the Quadruple Alliance begins
1720   The South Sea Bubble bursts
1720   War of the Quadruple Alliance ends
1722   *Louise Élisabeth d'Orléans and Louis, Prince of Asturias married*
1725   *Marie Leszczyńska and Louis XV married*
1727   *George I dies*
1727   *Reign of George II begins*
1727   Anglo–Spanish War begins
1727   *Louise Élisabeth and Anne Henriette de France born*
1729   Anglo–Spanish War ends

1730   *Peter II dies*
1737   *Caroline of Ansbach dies*
1738   *George III born*
1740   *Ivan VI born*
1740   The Irish Famine
1740   *Anna of Russia dies*
1740   *Charles VI dies*
1741   *Princess Elizabeth born*
1742   *Elizabeth of Russia and Alexei Razumovsky married*
1746   The Battle of Culloden
1749   *Princess Louisa born*
1751   *Frederick Louis, Prince of Wales, dies*
1754   *Louis XVI born*
1755   Lisbon earthquake kills 30,000
1756   Seven Years' War begins
1758   *Prince Augustus William of Prussia dies*
1759   *Anne, Princess Royal, dies*
1760   *George II dies*
1760   *Reign of George III begins*
1761   *George III and Charlotte of Mecklenburg-Strelitz married*
1762   *Elizabeth of Russia dies*
1762   *George IV born*
1763   Seven Years' War ends
1766   *Prince William Henry and Maria Walpole married*
1766   *Charlotte, Princess Royal, born*
1770   *Louis XVI and Marie Antoinette married*
1770   Captain James Cook discovers Botany Bay, Australia
1771   *Adolf Frederick of Sweden dies*
1771   *Louis XVIII and Marie Joséphine of Savoy married*
1771   *Prince Henry and Anne Horton married*
1772   *Johann Friedrich Struensee executed*
1772   *Queen Caroline Matilda imprisoned*
1772   Royal Marriages Act
1773   *Princess Sophia Matilda born*
1773   The Boston Tea Party

1811   The Regency begins
1813   The Battle of the Nations at Leipzig
1814   The First Bourbon Restoration
1815   The Hundred Days
1815   Napoleon defeated by Wellington at Waterloo
1815   The Napoleonic Wars end
1815   The Congress of Vienna concludes
1815   The Second Bourbon Restoration
1816   Prince Leopold of Saxe-Coburg-Saalfeld and Princess Charlotte of Wales married
1817   Princess Charlotte of Wales dies
1818   Charlotte of Mecklenburg-Strelitz dies
1818   Maria Isabel of Portugal dies
1818   William IV and Adelaide of Saxe-Meiningen married
1820   George III dies
1820   Reign of George IV begins
1820   The Pains and Penalties Bill
1821   Napoleon dies
1824   Louis XVIII dies
1830   George IV dies
1830   Reign of William IV begins
1830   The July Revolution in France
1830   The November Uprising against Russia
1832   Napoleon II dies
1837   William IV dies

Introduction

'This day, at half an Hour past Seven in the Morning, died our late most Gracious Sovereign Queen Anne, in the Fiftieth Year of Her Age and the Thirteenth of Her Reign.'[1]

And so, with those deceptively simple words, began the Georgian era. Powdered and preened, bewigged, bejewelled and bewitching, it is a period in history that has fascinated generations. From film to stage, catwalk to literature, architecture and beyond, the influence of the Georgian era can be felt everywhere. As the Age of Enlightenment flourished, great thinkers, writers, artists, engineers and reformers prospered whilst across Europe, kings, queens, emperors and empresses took to their thrones to conquer, to rule and to live lives that were never short on drama.

When Queen Anne died in her bed at Kensington Palace on 1 August 1714, the succession of the house of Stuart died with her, with neither heir nor spare waiting to warm the throne. More than a century after James became the first Stuart monarch of England, the country stood on the brink of a new era. In The Hague, George, Elector of Hanover, prepared to travel to his new kingdom and the curtain rose on a glittering age of social, cultural and political upheaval.

His place on the throne was assured by the 1701 Act of Settlement, prompted by the realization that the incumbent Stuart monarch, King William III, was unlikely to provide an heir. Facing the very real threat of Catholic restoration, Parliament moved swiftly to ensure a Protestant line of succession with the legislation.

The Act ruled that, should no Stuart heir survive, then the crown would pass to Sophia, Electress of Hanover or her successor. The Act also contained the vital clause that no Catholic could sit on the English throne and, should the heir or Sovereign marry a Catholic, then they would be removed from the line of succession.

George's path to the throne was a twisting one and, truth be told, the role was not one he welcomed, but like so many of the noble names we will meet in these pages, his duty came first. Under the terms of the Act of Settlement, the Elector of Hanover became the first King George of that period of British history better known today as *Georgian*. Of course, one didn't have to be named George to be a Georgian ruler and our gallop through the courts will take us through four Georges (one of whom was also Prince Regent) and all the way to William IV.

To our twenty-first century eyes, the Georgian kings can seem almost impossibly alien. They peer grandly down from canvases bearing the flourished signatures of some of the most illustrious names in eighteenth century art, wigs perfectly in place, models of privilege and propriety in their robes of state. What, though, of the people beneath the horsehair and silk; were they as human as the rest of us despite their pomp?

Although the Georgian court could never be described as uneventful, it certainly received a run from its money across the sea where the continental houses of Habsburg, Romanov and Bourbon flourished and, in some cases, fell. They were not, of course *Georgian* by name, but they are very much part of the history of the era and their stories feature here too. In these pages, we will journey through the European courts of the eighteenth and nineteenth century to meet some of the noble players who seem so grandly imposing up there in their gilded frames.

This is not a biography of European monarchy nor a history of the house of Hanover; it is a collection of stories from the courts of Europe that feature generous helpings of action, romance, scandal, intrigue and, every now and then, a good dollop of gore. Behind ancient walls and beneath glittering chandeliers the crowned heads of Europe cheated, lied, fell in love and pursued vendettas that would put the most full-blooded fiction to shame.

You will find the book split into four acts beginning in childhood and taking in marriage, scandal and death. In the timeline you will discover some of the events that shook the world during the era and for those ardent royal watchers who like to track their favourite families and even tick off their tombstones, dates of birth and death are also included wherever appropriate.

Both old and new style dates are listed where relevant, and the titles used in the text are those by which the characters are best known. In the case of George I, for instance, you will find him referred to primarily as George I, rather than the lengthy list of titles he acquired throughout his long and eventful life.

Some of these stories are legendary, immortalized on stage, screen and in literature. Others are perhaps less celebrated but no less fascinating, and the hardest part of assembling this volume was deciding what to leave out. With so much drama happening all over Europe, I do hope you will find something to entertain you!

So settle in your gallery seat as the curtain goes up on *Life in the Georgian Court* and be advised, some of these stories might not be suitable for those of a sensitive disposition.

Act One

Childhood

'It may be doubted, whether the pleasure of seeing children ripening into strength be not overbalanced by the pain of seeing some fall in the blossom...'

Samuel Johnson, 1750

What do you think of when you imagine the life of a royal child? If you answered privilege, travel, excitement and a world of wealth and luxury that few could even dream of, you are probably in the majority. Perhaps you might also picture public adoration, the best education money can buy and the certainty of a life where those in an exalted position can have anything, let alone *anybody*.

Though there will no doubt be any number of benefits inherent in being born into a royal house, even for a twenty-first century royal child, there will doubtless be something a little less idyllic lurking too. Press intrusion, the weight of expectation and the need to *do one's duty* are all in the woodpile but, for the royal youngsters of the long eighteenth century, there was certainly a lot more to childhood than the already fraught matter of just growing up. If modern children are at least afforded the time and training to ease into their public roles, such consideration was rarely given to the noble offspring of the Georgian era.

Almost as soon as they were born, a royal child could become a political pawn in the ruthless world of the marriage mart, where children as young as three were betrothed in hard-fought deals that secured territory and shored up alliances. A scarring dose of smallpox could prove fatal for the future prospects of a young princess just as an unambitious second son, happily pottering through childhood, could suddenly be thrust into the political spotlight by the death of an older brother. Some daughters might find themselves forever unmarried simply because it was the wish of their parents, their brothers forced into marriage to women where love was a distant dream. One thing all had in common was the fact that their duty was clear – the family business came above all else.

Of course, royal youngsters were children like any other, and on the far too common yet never less than tragic occasions when their lives were cut short, their parents were bereft as any would be. Sadly, politics all too often intervened in these young lives and in this chapter we will see some extreme examples of the fates that could befall royal children, such as the sons of France and Russia who faced cruel incarceration that ended in death, victims of events beyond their understanding. We will also meet unsuspecting brides and timid sons thrust onto a throne left cold by the death of a favoured brother.

Included here are vignettes of royal children who are perhaps not as famed as others and happily, not all of these tales end in tragedy. One thing all of these children have in common is that they were considered legitimate, though there are a wealth of illegitimate children waiting in the wings to have their stories told too!

Some of the youngsters who feature in this chapter will reappear in these pages as brides or grooms or even as they lay on their deathbeds many decades later. For now though, let us turn our spotlight on those children who were born to the noble houses of Europe and hear their very different stories.

An Era Begins

George I, King of Great Britain and Ireland (Hanover)
Osnabrück, Hanover, 28 May 1660–
Osnabrück, Hanover, 11 June 1727

It seems only proper that the first royal child to take the stage is the boy destined to become King of Great Britain, the first monarch of the era that took his name as its own and gave us one of the most extraordinary periods in European history.

At the moment of George's birth in Hanover, there was no Act of Settlement, no whisper of the end of the Stuart dynasty and no reason to suspect that the newborn son of Ernest Augustus, Duke of Brunswick-Lüneburg, and his wife, Sophia of the Palatinate, would one day rule over England. The territories he stood to inherit were less lofty though they were at least secure and war or diplomatic disaster aside, he could one day count on inheriting the lands controlled by his father and those uncles who had no heirs of their own.

Alongside his younger brother, Frederick Augustus, George was initially raised in Hanover without the benefit of his mother's presence. Sophia was in Italy recovering from illness but she kept up a constant correspondence with home, her letters easing the sting of her absence until she could return to Hanover in 1665. Once she was reunited with her children, she proved a devoted mother and was particularly proud of her mature and intelligent eldest son, thinking him a fine future ruler. However, when one of those all-important uncles died and the other two found brides, Sophia grew concerned that the teenage George might stand to inherit a vastly reduced territory.

Of course, it was ultimately to prove a moot point but what it *did* mean was that George's once assured future was now slightly less set in stone. Accordingly, it was decided that the young man should be prepared for the distinct possibility that he might actually have need of a career of some sort.

George now found there was less emphasis on the matter of ruling and leadership and more on the chance that he might one day need to fight to protect the territories he would inherit. With this in mind, it was decided that what George *really* needed was a taste of the army life. It is unthinkable to us now but in 1675, at only 15, he joined his father on a campaign in the Franco-Dutch War, to experience battle firsthand.

Happily for George, a fortunately timed death put paid to the fear that a career in the military might be his destiny. His uncles might have found brides but producing an heir was an entirely different matter and when another uncle died without male issue, George's future inheritance in Hanover was finally secured. Now 19, he no doubt felt some relief at this new certainty but fate held another twist and more than three decades later, it would catapult him onto the British throne.

The Princess of Variolation

Anne, Princess Royal (Hanover)

Hanover, Germany, 2 November 1709–
The Hague, The Netherlands, 12 January 1759

Five years before George, Elector of Hanover, travelled to England to ring in the start of the Georgian era, he became grandfather to a newborn girl, courtesy of his son, George, Prince of Wales, later king of Great Britain and his bride, the ill-fated Caroline of Ansbach. History was commemorated in the girl's very name and she was baptized *Anne*, in honour of the Stuart queen whose death propelled the Elector and his family onto the British throne for generations.

There was nothing particularly unusual about the little girl's upbringing and like others of her station and gender, she was raised in preparation for marriage. Though bright, playful and particularly gifted in music, it is not for her musical acumen that Anne's childhood left a mark. Instead, the little girl played a role in a tragic drama that engulfed tens of thousands throughout the eighteenth century, including plenty of royals.

The relationship between Anne's grandparents and parents was fractious and hostile and eventually the feud between father and son exploded into vitriol. When the Prince of Wales was exiled to Leicester House, Caroline chose to go with him, leaving their children in the custody of the king.

For a child so young, this must have been devastating and further sadness was to come in 1720 when Anne contracted smallpox. For hundreds of thousands of victims the disease proved deadly and even for those who survived, the side effects could range from blindness to disfiguring scars. Faced with Anne's critical condition the king thawed and allowed her parents to visit. Happily, Anne survived the infection, though for the rest of her life she bore the scars it left behind.

For Anne's mother, her daughter's battle struck a little too close to home. At the age of three, Caroline had lost her own father to the disease and watching Anne almost suffer the same fate galvanized her into action. As is so often the case with parents touched by the suffering of a child, Caroline determined that she must find some way to help in the fight against smallpox and devoted herself to this worthwhile pursuit.

Eventually Caroline's studies encountered the practice of variolation, an early form of inoculation, and a procedure that was still in its infancy in England though widely used in other parts of the world. Caroline became aware of variolation thanks to its promotion by Lady Mary Wortley Montagu, who had first encountered the practice in Turkey. Lady Mary's own family had been touched by the disease and, like Caroline, she was on a mission to fight smallpox, but variolation was not an easy sell to western physicians.

The practice of variolation involved taking a very small amount of smallpox-infected tissue and introducing it into the body of a healthy patient. The result was a very mild infection and, from then on, invaluable immunity. Lady Mary had Charles Maitland, a Scottish surgeon she had encountered in Turkey, as her medical expert and when Caroline wished to prove the efficacy of variolation, it was to Maitland that she turned.

Caroline established an experiment that took place at Newgate Prison on 9 August 1721, when six convicts were promised a pardon in return for agreeing to serve as Maitland's guinea pigs. The procedure proved to be a success and Caroline was greatly heartened, determined that no more of her loved ones would suffer as her father and daughter had done.

Despite the success of the procedure on the adult prisoners, however, she was still reluctant to subject her children to the treatment without proper testing and to this end, she funded variolation for a number of orphans in London. Though her motives might have been self-interested rather than *entirely* altruistic, the results cannot be underestimated and no doubt many lives were saved as a result of the publicity her interest brought to the treatment.

Suitably convinced, Caroline requested that Maitland variolate the royal children and he agreed, carrying out the procedure swiftly and without complications. Unwittingly, Princess Anne's suffering contributed to an enthusiasm for variolation that saved many lives and certainly raised awareness of this ancient Eastern process for battling the scourge of smallpox. Naturally, with an illustrious lady such as Caroline of Ansbach championing the procedure, it was soon quite the done thing. In time, variolation was no longer regarded with the suspicion and outright hostility that had once greeted it and instead became a highly popular procedure in England.

Anne's own life was, happily, not disadvantaged by her brush with smallpox. Not one to be cowed, she spent her convalescence immersed in her studies and recovered to live a further forty years, the legacy left by her infection one that had an immense impact on smallpox treatment throughout the land her family ruled.

Before Frederick Was Great

Frederick II, King of Prussia, known as Frederick the Great. (Hohenzollern)
Berlin, Prussia, 24 January 1712–Potsdam, Prussia, 17 August 1786

Like all children, those raised in royal households were shaped in adulthood by the experiences they knew during their formative years. For some, such as a certain unfortunate Bourbon, the experiences of the nursery left them ill-prepared for the turbulent world they were one day to inherit yet for others, education instilled a sense of unshakeable self-worth that would set the stage for the day when they assumed that all-important leading role on the throne.

As we will see later, the young dauphin who would one day die on the guillotine as the deposed Louis XVI, spent his early years in timid, good behaviour, but the child who would become Frederick the Great barely knew the meaning of the word *timid*.

As son of Frederick William I of Prussia, and his wife, Sophia Dorothea of Hanover, Frederick, known as *Fritz*, was the grandson of George I and nephew of George II. The house of Hohenzollern had already buried two infant heirs and his healthy birth was the source of enormous celebration. Frederick William and Sophia Dorothea must have felt an immeasurable sense of relief both emotionally and politically when the healthy Frederick came along. With his line of succession assured, the little boy's grandfather, Frederick I, duly died in 1713 and Frederick William took the throne, leaving his infant son, the new crown prince, as the next in line.

Frederick William was determined that his long-awaited son should not be a cosseted royal but instead forged into a disciplined ruler. Frederick William did not want a spoiled, privileged son, he envisioned an heir well-prepared to rule the Prussian territories when his time came. The king was not a gentle father and, believing his son to be effete and unmanly, took delight in disciplining him in front of others, a bullying streak that would eventually end in tragedy.

To educate his son, Frederick William turned to his own childhood tutor, Marthe de Rocoulle. She had learned to be patient whilst caring for Frederick William, who enjoyed pranking her, whether it be by hiding or even, on occasion, swallowing shoe buckles! For a lady approaching her dotage, caring for Frederick must have seemed like the full time job to end all full time jobs and, as he grew more wilful, it was decided that he should move on to sterner tutors and let Marthe grow old peacefully.

Frederick's father directed that his son should be strictly educated in practical and religious matters with no time for arts and philosophy, but the crown prince was not a timid and obedient child and practical and religious matters were *not* at the top of his agenda. Fiercely intelligent and with a passion for art and literature, Frederick endured terrible and repeated beatings that his father hoped would thrash some sense and discipline into him. Instead the little boy became secretive and withdrawn, nurturing a silent hatred for Frederick William that grew ever deeper. With each new humiliation his desperation for freedom increased and he dreamed of the day when he might escape the tyrannical influence of his father and see something of the world.

Perhaps the most influential figure in the young man's life was Jacques Duhan de Jandun, Frederick's tutor in all matters scientific. When he was appointed, the king believed Duhan would be the ideal figure to ensure the pragmatic education he intended for his child, yet there was much more to the new tutor than that.

In fact, far from keeping Fritz's mind occupied and safely away from matters of art and letters, Duhan introduced studies of the classics and continental literature to quench his charge's thirst for knowledge. He provided the boy with a secretly procured library numbering three thousand volumes and it was kept hidden away at the Schlossfreiheit, well out of the unsuspecting king's reach. Later, this hidden library would result in Duhan's temporary imprisonment but it can hardly be doubted that this clandestine education played an enormous role in Fritz's intellectual development.

Frederick's childhood ended once and for all when, at the age of 18, he and his friend, Hans Hermann von Katte, a Lieutenant in the Prussian army, secretly planned an escape to England. News of the scheme reached Frederick William and he had the two young men arrested and imprisoned in the fortress of Küstrin. Here the young Fritz was forced to witness his friend's execution, with von Katte beheaded in front of him. Frederick's loathing of his father was sealed once and for all, yet it would be another decade before he would finally be rid of the man who had treated him so badly.

The Infant Prince

Prince George William of Great Britain (Hanover)

London, England, 2 November 1717–

London, England, 6 February 1718

The royal courts of the eighteenth century seethed with intrigue and passion, with secrets and plots. With so much at stake in such a politicized world, it was perhaps inevitable in the heightened power plays of the Georgian court that some of our royal children would be dragged into the drama, used as innocent pawns in the political games of those who hungered for power. The sad case of Prince George William proved that even the youngest babe might land at the epicentre of a hurricane of familial resentment and the four Georges were *nothing* if not fond of the odd nasty feud.

Born at St James's Palace, George was the son of Caroline of Ansbach and George, Prince of Wales. The child's life was tragically short but even in the three months he lived, he witnessed plenty of drama from his cradle as a situation that should have brought celebration instead led to heartache.

The birth of George William was the cause of enormous rejoicing not only for the baby's family, but also for the nation. After all, it was years since a royal child had been born in England and there was much celebration at the news of his safe delivery, with this newborn Hanoverian unquestionably an *English* boy.

The baptism of the little prince was set for the month after his birth, the ceremony to be officiated by William Wake, Archbishop of Canterbury, and conducted in Caroline's bedchamber. The king decided that *he* would serve as godparent, alongside Thomas Pelham-Holles, 1st Duke of Newcastle, and Diana Beauclerk, Duchess of St Albans. However, as has been the case in any number of families, this happy occasion proved to be incendiary for the already stretched relations between the newborn's father and the proud new grandparent.

The Prince and Princess of Wales compiled a shortlist of names for their new treasure that, fatally, did not include the name George. Likewise, they compiled a list of likely godparents on which neither Newcastle nor St Albans were anywhere to be seen. As a new grandfather, the king turned to his advisors for their suggestions and it was agreed that his choice of godparents would stand, regardless of what the boy's parents might wish. Likewise, he decided that, whatever the Prince and Princess of Wales thought about it, George was really the *only* appropriate name for the new baby. As the king knew it would be, the news of Newcastle's involvement was a shattering blow to the Prince of Wales who considered the duke a long-standing enemy. He entreated his father to change his mind yet his pleas fell on deaf ears and the smug Newcastle was in no hurry to withdraw.

Although far from happy with this imposition, the new parents decided to honour the king's wishes and at least *attempt* to keep their relationship on an even keel. However, at the baptism tempers flared dramatically with a furious altercation taking place between Newcastle and the Prince of Wales. Things came perilously close to a physical confrontation and once the ceremony was ended, Newcastle hurried to the king and told him that the Prince of Wales had threatened him to a duel.

Despite George's furious denials that any such thing had happened, the Prince of Wales was ordered out of St James's Palace and his wife went with him. They were not allowed to take their children, the newborn George William and his sisters, and were forced to take up residence at Leicester House without them. This cruel decision cut Caroline particularly deeply as she had been forced to leave her eldest son, Frederick, at home in Hanover when she travelled to England. To now have her other children so close and yet so far away was a devastating reminder of that terrible moment of separation.

Crippled with anxiety, Caroline made secret trips to see her son and daughters until January when George finally thawed just a little, allowing Caroline access to them. When George William fell ill the following month, the king had him moved to Kensington Palace and, concerned that the little boy might not live, allowed both parents to be reunited with their son.

Sadly the reunion was cut short by the tragic death of the little boy. His mother was bereft, believing his separation from her was to blame for his sad fate though in fact, the cause of his death was a polyp on the heart. This tragic event did nothing to mend the deep rift between the Prince of Wales and his father, their already tense relationship stretched even further. Caroline was allowed far freer access to Anne following the little girl's near-fatal brush with smallpox but she felt the loss of her baby keenly. Whether the heartbroken Caroline ever recovered from George William's death is debatable; it was a tragedy she was to feel for many years to come.

The Twins of Versailles

Louise Élisabeth and Anne Henriette de France (Bourbon)
Versailles, France, 14 August 1727–Versailles, France, 6 December 1759
(Louise Élisabeth) and Versailles, France, 10 February 1752 (Henriette)

On 14 August 1727, their first children, identical twin girls were born at Versailles to Louis XV and his wife, Marie Leszczyńska. These *Filles des France* were not, however, exactly what the world had been waiting for and their childhoods serve as a reminder of just how young a girl might find herself plunged into the marriage market in the world of the eighteenth century monarchy

When the royal couple announced Marie's pregnancy, hopes were high that the firstborn child would be a boy, thus securing the line of succession. However, when the girls made their appearance, their birth was greeted with somewhat mute celebrations by court and public alike, all of whom were waiting for a dauphin. The throne of France was a particularly desirable one, so the last thing that was needed was yet another uncertain succession and until a boy appeared, things at Versailles were politically far from ideal.

Still, regardless of what their court and country might have thought, Louis and Marie were understandably besotted with the new arrivals. Though he doted on both, Louis formed a particular attachment to Louise Élisabeth, whom he nicknamed *Babette*. Their education was entrusted to Marie Isabelle de Rohan, Duchess of Tallard, who took over role as governess to the Bourbon household from her grandmother. The duchess cared for a great many royal children, as well as establishing an abiding friendship with the king himself.

Under the watchful eye of the duchess the little girls soon flourished. Bright, charming and full of energy, it was not long before their parents became aware of just how valuable these young ladies could be in the world of courtly marriage. After all, the right match for a royal daughter could forge invaluable territorial and political links, and the wealthy and powerful house of Bourbon certainly made for an attractive proposition.

It was decided that the girls would continue the long tradition of Catholic alliances and diplomatic feelers were put out to identify suitable spouses for the *Filles des France*. Having come from a somewhat minor family herself, the queen was particularly conscious of the difference a well-matched marriage could make. The house of Leszczyński was far from the centre of the royal universe and the perception that she had overstepped her place in snagging a Bourbon king had serious implications for Marie's life at court, as we will learn later. She didn't intend to see her own lack of popularity visited on her daughters and was at pains to ensure that the search for appropriate husbands was a model of propriety.

The girls were barely into double figures when Louise Élisabeth was betrothed to the Infante Philip of Spain, son of King Philip V and Elisabeth Farnese. Though the French court was ambivalent, Louis was delighted with the very safe prospect presented by this fairly pedestrian match. It was a politically astute union too, intended to strengthen relations with Spain and banish any ill-will that still remained following the broken betrothal between Louis XV and Infanta Mariana Victoria years earlier.

The young couple were married by proxy on 26 August 1739. Thrust from childhood into a bewildering new world, the heartbroken Louise left Versailles immediately, separated from her beloved twin for the first time in their short lives. With Babette bound for married life and her waiting husband at Alcalá de Henares, childhood was over.

Of course, this left one unmarried twin at Versailles and no obvious suitors on the horizon. A talented instrumentalist, Henriette lost herself in her lessons, music filling the silence where she had once enjoyed the company of her sister. There was, however, another companion in her life and when she was in her early teens, a friendship with her cousin, Louis Philippe d'Orléans, Duke of Chartres, turned to love.

Henriette turned to her father and petitioned for leave to marry the young man. At first it seemed that the king might agree until he took the problem to his most trusted advisor, Cardinal Fleury. Fleury was unequivocal in his decision that the king must reject his daughter's heartfelt requests. Such a marriage would bring the house of Orléans within a whisker of the throne itself and, with Fleury's whole life devoted to furthering Bourbon interests, such a situation could not be allowed to arise.

When her father refused to permit the marriage, Henriette retreated yet further into her musical studies; perhaps tellingly, she never married, whether for love *or* politics.

The Nameless One

Ivan VI, Emperor and Autocrat of All the Russias (Brunswick-Bevern)
St Petersburg, Russia, 23 August 1740–
Shlisselburg, Russia, 16 July 1764

Later in these pages we will meet the ill-fated Louis XVII, the boy king who never sat on the throne of France, but decades before Louis was born, another child ruler never quite made it as far as wearing the crown. He was Ivan VI, *the nameless one*, a boy who was little more than a pawn in the political ambitions of others and suffered a heartbreaking fate at the hands of those who fought for power.

Ivan was born as the son of Prince Antony Ulrich of Brunswick–Lüneburg and the woman who would rule as Grand Duchess Anna Leopoldovna of Russia, the granddaughter of Ivan V and niece of the no-nonsense Empress Anna. When Ivan was only weeks old, the ailing empress named him as the heir to the throne of Russia, appointing her favourite courtier, Ernst Johann von Biron, Duke of Courland, to serve as regent until Ivan was old enough to rule.

Of course, whilst the feared and powerful empress lived, everyone was quick to agree that this would be an admirable arrangement yet almost as soon as Anna died in 1740, things took a most dramatic turn. Within a month Biron was placed under arrest and wrenched from the throne which he had lobbied so hard to win. Though his sentence was exile, not death, his influence was snuffed out in the blink of an eye and little Ivan's triumphant mother, Anna Leopoldovna, took over the mantle of regent on behalf of her son.

For now, the three-month-old Ivan had nothing whatsoever to fear, but the power plays of the Romanov court were turning and twisting and in December 1741 another coup swept his mother from the seat of power. Anna was thrust unceremoniously aside by the newly enthroned Empress Elizabeth, daughter of Peter the Great. Elizabeth's surprisingly bloodless coup began a rule that would last for two decades and Ivan and his entire family were placed under arrest in the fortress at Dünamünde in Riga.

Neither court nor military were sad to see the back of the inexperienced Anna Leopoldovna and the family were not detained for long before they were allowed to plan a residence in Brunswick. However, the infant Ivan's fate was to take a turn for the worse, based on nothing more concrete than the convoluted plot of two French agents to discredit a woman named Natalia Fyodorovna Lopukhina.

A popular lady at the court of Empress Anna, Lopukhina had plenty of friends in high places and enjoyed no small influence thanks to her enduring friendship with Anna Bestuzheva, sister-in-law of vice-chancellor, Aleksey Bestuzhev. Bestuzhev was a great supporter of Austria, France's political rival, and therein was the thorny problem. He had the ear of the empress and if he were to encourage Russian support of Austria, things might go very badly for France in all sorts of ways.

Soon gossip reached the empress that Lopukhina and her son had been overheard discussing the restoration of Ivan VI. Lopukhina and Anna Bestuzheva were taken into custody and subjected to torture yet neither was able to spill the beans on a planned coup for the simple reason that, idle gossip aside, there was nothing to tell. However, the influential vice-chancellor was dragged into the mess and risked his position and power, whilst the two unfortunate ladies were sent to Siberia, their tongues cut out before they went.

All of this had dire consequences for Ivan and just two months before his fourth birthday, Empress Elizabeth already regarded him and his family with fresh suspicion. Although the Lopukhina affair had provided no proof of any serious attempt to reinstate the deposed emperor on the throne, the empress decided that it was a risk she just couldn't take and embarked on an unthinkable scheme.

Ivan was taken from his family and sent to Kholmogory on the White Sea, where he would remain for what was left of his childhood. The little boy who had reportedly been full of life and cheer was placed in a windowless cell, where he knew no friends and had little access to the world outside. Allowed into the grounds only by night and under heavy guard, it was hardly surprising that, like the little dauphin imprisoned in France so many years later, his health and wellbeing soon began to suffer.

Locked away so early in his physical and mental development Ivan was given little education, though he did have some ability to read and write. It is heartbreaking to imagine a child torn from his family and all that was dear to him and thrust into an isolated, strict world in which even grown and hardened criminals would struggle to cope.

Despite his situation, Ivan was acutely aware of his birthright and referred to himself as *emperor*. Even as the years passed and his mental state grew increasingly disturbed, he never forgot his title though of course, in the bleak cell at Kholmogory, it was a word without meaning. Under constant guard, this *nameless one* lived a life of lonely solitude from which he would never escape.

The child saw only his jailers and his location was whispered about even if it was never confirmed; however, for Elizabeth up on the Romanov throne, even whispers were too much to stand. He and his mother, who died in 1746, were, to all intents and purposes, written out of the country's history. As with all the most juicy gossip, this just served to make the whispers grow louder and Elizabeth took action against Ivan once more, intending to send him so far away that he would soon be forgotten by all.

When Ivan was sixteen he was moved to Shlüsselburg, the forbidding fortress that would be his last home. Here he would be held in manacles, his existence one of lonely cruelty. After the empress died, her successors met with the prisoner yet still he remained in shackles, treated as a madman and denied his freedom. It is hardly surprising that neither Peter III nor Catherine the Great saw fit to release him; after all, what monarch would set free the one man who could lay claim to their own crown? Instead the boy grew into a young man known as *Grigorii*, labelled a lunatic and left to rot.

It might seem that Elizabeth had been somewhat paranoid in her absolute certainty that someone would attempt to free the young man yet, eventually, that is *exactly* what happened. That man was Lieutenant Vasilii Mirovich, a guard at Shlüsselburg. His intention was to free Ivan, by now in his twenties, and use him as a figurehead for a revolt against Catherine. With the support of many of the guards at the fortress, it was even possible that he might succeed.

Sadly it was not to be and when Ivan's jailers heard the commotion as Mirovich's men seized control of Shlüsselburg, they acted immediately. When the jailers stormed into Ivan's cell and attacked him with their swords, the frail young man stood no chance and died there in the bleak, tiny room that had been his whole world, never to take his place on the throne of Russia.

It was the final act in a dark and tragic chapter in the history of our eighteenth century royal children and decades later, as revolution swept through France, another boy would find himself ripped from his family and confined to a life without affection. One can only mourn for the fate of Ivan, the little boy who was a prisoner almost from the moment of his birth.

A Forgotten Princess

Princess Elizabeth of Great Britain

London, England, 10 January 1741–
Kew, Surrey, England, 4 September 1759

The daughters of the house of Hanover were not, it must be said, the most robust young ladies ever to reside in the palaces of England. One of the most delicate of all the girls was undoubtedly Princess Elizabeth Caroline, a girl who is little remembered today. Her life was short and not particularly eventful, the inevitable outcome no less tragic for its predictability.

In 1741, Princess Elizabeth was born at Norfolk House, St James's Square, to Frederick, Prince of Wales, and Augusta of Saxe-Gotha. Her grandparents were George II and Caroline of Ansbach, and in keeping with tradition and expectation, the newborn princess was christened in the first few weeks of her life by Thomas Secker, at that time Bishop of Oxford and later Archbishop of Canterbury.

Bright and cheery, the little girl was, nevertheless, physically weak. A gentle child adored by her siblings, Princess Elizabeth enjoyed nothing better than indulging in theatrical entertainments at home, battling her own infirmity to do so. There was no question that one so frail would enter into the royal marriage market and at the age of eighteen, the princess fell ill with an inflammation of the bowels from which she would never recover.

It was the last and most serious blow in all her years of ill health and despite being born into what should have been the most powerful house in the land, nothing could be done to save the unfortunate young lady from her suffering.

Within days of falling ill, Princess Elizabeth passed away at Kew Palace. As her family mourned, the unfortunate girl was laid to rest in Westminster Abbey, her name fading into history.

An Untold Life

Princess Louisa of Great Britain

London, England, 19 March 1749–
London, England, 13 May 1768

Along with her short-lived sister, Princess Elizabeth of Great Britain, Princess Louisa is one of those royal children who were destined to be somewhat forgotten by history, eclipsed by their longer-living siblings. Neither Elizabeth nor Louisa lived long enough to make a mark upon the world, and it is precisely this that has caught my attention. Including them within these pages is my small contribution to ensuring that these two daughters of the house of Hanover are not entirely forgotten.

Louisa was born at Leicester House, Westminster, to Frederick, Prince of Wales, and Augusta of Saxe-Gotha. As grandchild to George II and Caroline of Ansbach her birth could hardly have been more illustrious, yet all the privilege in the world would not be enough to save the girl from a short life. Unlike Elizabeth, Louisa appeared to be a healthy child and this made her sudden decline and early death all the more shocking.

In keeping with her good health, Princess Louisa lived a relatively normal childhood, proving herself to be a bright and inquisitive little girl. Charming, intelligent and popular with her siblings, it would seem that she had a particular closeness to Elizabeth and when she died in Louisa's tenth year, the little girl's own health took an alarming turn for the worst.

Without the buoying influence and friendship of her elder sister, the princess grew increasingly weak and frail. Eventually she took to her bed and it became apparent to her family that she would not be able to fully enter into court life. Although marriage plans had been discussed with the Danish house of Oldenburg, Louisa's ill health made the prospect of travel an impossibility and instead it was her sister, Caroline Matilda, who would undertake that ill-fated match.

Weakened beyond recovery, Louisa died at Carlton House aged just 19. The exact circumstances of her death were not recorded but, given its prolonged nature, it is perhaps likely that she was a victim of tuberculosis.

On 16 May, the St James's Chronicle recorded that 'Yesterday Morning, about Ten of the Clock, died here [Carlton House], after a long and painful Illness, her Royal Highness the Princess Louisa Anne, his majesty's second Sister, to the great Grief of their Majesties, and all the Royal Family.'[2] It is a rare mention of the unfortunate young princess, so eclipsed by her illustrious relatives.

The Boy Who Would Be King

Louis XVI, King of France and Navarre (Bourbon)

Versailles, France, 23 August 1754–

Paris, France, 21 January 1793

It is perhaps an inevitable fact of life that when one becomes the only king of France to die on the guillotine, one tends to be remembered only for that.

There was, of course, much more to Louis XVI than the way he died and the timid king who met his fate on the scaffold was forged in a childhood that was far from idyllic.

As we will see when we peek in at Louis and Marie Antoinette's marriage, the bride endured some unimaginable experiences in order to win the approval of the house of Bourbon yet for Louis, things were a little more straightforward. Certainly, unlike the young archduchess who was to be his wife, there was no *question* of unanesthetized dental work for the Dauphin of France.

Louis Auguste de France, Duke of Berry, was born to Louis, Dauphin of France, and Maria Josepha of Saxony, in the luxurious surroundings of the Palace of Versailles. When Louis was born his brother, Louis Joseph, Duke of Burgundy (we shall call him Burgundy, since there are so many boys named Louis in this tale!), was just shy of 3 years old and was the apple of his family's eye. Timid and unassuming, Louis's shy nature meant that it was easy for his parents to unthinkingly sideline him in favour of the charming and vivacious Burgundy and even their governess seemed to prefer the older boy, with all in agreement that he was close to being the perfect son. Even the young Louis idolized his sibling and when a playroom accident left Burgundy in failing health, his younger brother was his devoted carer.

Whilst playing with friends the intrepid Burgundy fell from a rocking horse and what should have been an inconsequential injury instead led to a diagnosis of tuberculosis of the bone. As the condition of the once lively little boy grew ever more serious, it became apparent to his distraught family that the duke would not recover, surely a horrific prospect for any parent. His fate was made all the more poignant when one considers that the couple had already buried two children, a son and a daughter, less than a decade earlier. At the thought of losing another child prematurely they were cut to the quick and when the beloved 9-year-old boy died, retreated beneath a veil of grief.

Suddenly, with the death of Burgundy, the unprepared Louis was heir to the throne of France. Whilst his late brother had already begun to prepare for the role that awaited him, Louis was not so lucky and now his education took on a vital importance. As his parents mourned their lost child, Louis withdrew into himself under the tutelage of his father's trusted friend, the

Duke of la Vauguyon, the man charged with the education of the future king of France.

Like all children, Louis could be a lazy student but when the subject under discussion interested him, he was a model pupil. He was a deeply intelligent child and given not only to academic pursuits, but to outdoor pastimes too. Indeed, no doubt he would have been a delight to any parents yet to the bereaved Louis and Maria Josepha, his qualities were eclipsed by the memory of the idealized son they had lost too soon.

Under la Vauguyon, Louis underwent intensive education in the business of being a king. This formal training was highly traditional in nature, reflecting the perceived benefits of an absolutist monarchy and Louis absorbed it all, just as his father might wish. Of course, such traditional training would prove entirely unsuitable when Louis stood before the National Convention and tried to account for himself and his monarchy but he was not raised to question the status quo, only to enforce it.

As history will tell, when the French Revolution came knocking at the door of the house of Bourbon, that same ignored little boy, by now Louis XVI, failed to act decisively. Instead he remained circumspect, looking to others to make the more forceful moves and when they did not, he simply had nothing to draw on. It is tempting to speculate that the king who simply could not muster the force of character to meet the Revolution head on was born out of that house of grief and parental disinterest and to wonder what might have happened had Burgundy lived to take the crown.

Somewhere within the adult Louis there still lurked that child seeking approval: timid, polite and afraid to push himself forward for fear of causing offence. Utterly overwhelmed by the turbulent world in which he found himself, Louis's upbringing was to prove pivotal in the way he chose to meet the crisis that was Revolution.

A 'far from pretty' Princess

Charlotte, Princess Royal (Hanover)

London, England, 29 September 1766–
Ludwigsburg, Baden-Württemberg, Germany, 5 October 1828

There are many daughters of the house of Hanover and all would have made a deserving subject here. Indeed, whole books have been written devoted to these ladies and had I chosen to include them all, there would have been little space for anyone else. Instead, I selected a small number whose stories touched me for one reason or another. Some of them saved lives or reached illustrious social heights, whilst others died young and one or two have, over time, been virtually forgotten. Although not all of the daughters of Hanover appear in these pages, Charlotte, Princess Royal, will certainly pop up again and though her childhood was not remarkable, it illustrates all too starkly just how swiftly a favoured child's lustre can fade.

Charlotte was the fourth child and first daughter of George III and Charlotte of Mecklenburg-Strelitz. After welcoming three sons to their growing household, the royal family were ecstatic when the queen was delivered of a girl and she was christened amid much rejoicing by Thomas Secker, by now the Archbishop of Canterbury. Among her adoring godparents was our previous acquaintance, the short-lived Princess Louisa, who shared George and Charlotte's joy when they welcomed the new princess to their family.

Being a princess, however, is not all about adoration and privilege and even as they celebrated her birth, the king and queen were in no doubt that their new daughter would one day make someone an important wife. Accordingly, Charlotte's education began in early infancy, and this inquisitive, intelligent child excelled in her academic studies but one thing she had no particular enthusiasm for was marriage. Although she reluctantly agreed to all the diversions and entertainments required of her, Charlotte's true love was the schoolroom and her burgeoning enthusiasm for natural sciences.

As the sole girl among boys, the young princess found herself in a rather elevated position within the royal nursery. Here she enjoyed being the centre of attention but as more daughters eventually came along, Charlotte's undisputed central place came under threat. However, if the little girl was concerned she hardly showed it, instead happy to continue her studies in the care of her nurse, Mary Dacres, and governess, Lady Charlotte Finch.

Lady Finch proved a kindred spirit and shared with the young princess her love of botany. It soon became a passion for the girl, who was never happier than when she was wandering around the gardens at Kew, losing herself in the verdant surroundings and studying the specimens there.

Whilst it is quite one thing to share your nursery with your sisters, however, it is quite another to be unfavourably compared to them and in a world where marriages were brokered on all manner of factors, looks were not to be underestimated. Unhappily for Charlotte, not only was she not considered the prettiest of the daughters of George and Charlotte, she was also unfortunate enough to be told so.

On a visit to the royal nursery, Lady Mary Coke, famed for her waspish observations and unflinching commentary, decided that 5-year-old Charlotte was 'far from pretty'.[3] Her younger sister, Augusta Sophia, was 'rather pretty, but not so well as she was last year'[4] which can hardly be said to be a resounding compliment. On this occasion, perhaps due to her tender years, Charlotte did not lose her occasionally hot temper. It may be that she was thankfully too young to appreciate the unkindness of the judgment or perhaps she simply did not care for such things at such a young age, but as the years passed and she proved herself to be a woman of keen intellect and insight, a judgment made on childhood prettiness became less and less important.

By the time she was a young woman, Charlotte had bigger things on her mind and, when the Princess Royal finally set her sights on a husband, she chose a man with scandal in his past.

A Scandalous Babe

Princess Sophia Matilda of Gloucester (Hanover)

London, England, 29 May 1773–
Blackheath, Kent, England, 29 November 1844

You would be forgiven for thinking that, to win a place in this rundown of royal children, one must have lived an unhappy or, at the very least, *short* life. I am happy to redress the balance somewhat with the story of Princess Sophia Matilda of Gloucester. Born into scandal, this particular girl grew into a well-loved lady of some note.

In 1766 William Henry, Duke of Gloucester and Edinburgh and brother to George III, underwent a secret marriage ceremony to Maria Walpole, the Dowager Countess Waldegrave. Though her title might sound very illustrious, Maria had been born illegitimate and whilst her parents lived together as husband and wife, they never actually bothered to make their union official. Add to this the fact that Maria was a woman of no rank before her marriage *and* a widow too, and there was no way that she would have been considered an acceptable bride for the duke. For this reason, the wedding between William and Maria was kept a closely guarded secret and remained so for a pretty impressive six years. However, when Maria fell pregnant with Sophia, the couple decided that the time had come to tell the truth, recognizing that legitimizing their child was more important than George III's delicate feelings.

Upon learning of this illicit marriage, George felt a deep sense of betrayal that his brother had kept the secret for so long. The rift between king and duke would last for years and carried with it echoes of another feud within the family, when the scandalous marriage of *another* royal brother, Prince Henry, Duke of Cumberland and Strathearn, prompted the introduction of the Royal Marriages Act in 1772. Unable to shake the sense that William had wilfully betrayed him, George put in place a ruling that the duke, his wife and whatever family might result from their marriage should not be admitted to the royal household. However, in accordance with protocol and perhaps in an effort to mend the fractured sibling relationship, when Maria went into labour, word was sent to the king and queen to let them know that the new arrival was pending.

In the *Authentic and Impartial Memoirs of Her Late Majesty* (1819), it is recorded that:

'Previous to the delivery of the Duchess, the usual notice was sent to the King, requesting he would direct the proper officers to attend the birth, to prevent any future doubts; but no notice was taken.'[5]

When this message was ignored there can have been little lingering doubt that George intended to remain true to his word. With the pomp, ceremony and celebration of a royal christening denied to them, the new parents instead arranged a private baptism for their daughter with some family and friends in attendance, performed by Charles Moss, Bishop of St David's. Not all of the royal family shared the king's unhappiness and both Princess Amelia and Prince Henry, that other scandalous brother, were in attendance. The occasion *was* reported in the press, yet it would have been an easy event to miss:

> 'On Saturday evening the new-born Princess, daughter of the Royal Highnesses the Duke and Duchess of Gloucester, was privately baptized by the Lord Bishop of St. Davids, at Gloucester House, by the name of Sophia Matilda.'[6]

Once the little girl was christened, the family went overseas and established a home in Rome. Despite being exiled from court, the princess lived the life expected of a young lady and although it would be heartening to report that the king bore no ill will to the little girl herself, sadly this was not the case. She was not awarded the title of Royal Highness and though parliament put provision in place for her care should her father die, no such allowance was made during her life. Once Sophia's beloved brother, William, was born, George did arrange for the children to be cared for by a governess, but this was a meagre gesture and there can be little doubt that, as the years passed, George remained furious at the perceived deception his brother had perpetrated.

Eventually time seemed to work its magic and the king thawed somewhat and invited the duke and duchess to return to England. Here he found that his little niece had matured into a young lady of culture, intelligence and charm, loved by all who knew her. Although she had none of the fashionable gowns and jewels of her peers she nevertheless made her debut in honour of the king's birthday at the age of 17, a child no longer.

Sadly, the experience was not a happy one for Sophia, who found herself treated with rudeness and disinterest by those present at the ball. It was an inauspicious start to her life in London yet Sophia was not cowed. Little bothered by such indifference, she met it with grace and dignity, her popularity over the years that followed more than making up for that unhappy debut.

The Lost Dauphin

Louis XVII, King of France and Navarre (Bourbon)
Versailles, France, 27 March 1785–Paris, France, 8 June 1795

It would seem that all too often stories that feature Marie Antoinette and Louis XVII end in tragedy, and this tale is certainly more tragic than most. At the age of four, Louis Charles, the little boy who had been titled Duke of Normandy since birth, found himself as heir to the French throne, catapulted into the role of dauphin on the death of his seven year old brother, Louis Joseph, in 1789. The timing could not have been worse and though the forces of the French Revolution were already gathering, the tragic direction of the little boy's life could hardly be imagined.

When Louis Charles was born at Versailles to Louis XVI and Marie Antoinette, the news was met with great celebration as the queen had finally fulfilled her duty, providing an heir and the all-important spare. Breaking with tradition, Marie Antoinette delivered her son without the usual crowds in attendance, instead having been permitted a private labour, with those who would normally witness the occasion waiting in a neighbouring room. As the healthy infant was passed into the arms of his adoring mother, the court celebrated and Versailles was a most joyful place to be.

Cared for initially by Marie Antoinette's close friend, Yolande de Polastron, Duchess of Polignac and his beloved nurse, Agathe de Rambaud, the charming little boy was educated in the ways of court. He was well-liked by his carers and loved them in return though like his father before him, in the early years of Louis's life his parents were often distracted by the debilitating illness suffered by his brother, Louis Joseph.

Quite *unlike* his father though, the little boy did not encounter the wall of parental indifference that had marked Louis XVI's own childhood. Louis and Marie Antoinette left their youngest son in no doubt of their love for him and for the little boy, life was good. He had fine surroundings, an excellent education and the doting adoration of Madame de Rambaud, who was his constant shadow throughout infancy.

Just months after Louis Joseph's death in 1789, however, life changed for the new dauphin and his family. Transported from Versailles to the Tuileries Palace, the royal family's surroundings and horizons began to shrink. Travel was forbidden, visitors and court intrigues dwindled to nothing and from all sides they were watched. Of course, it is possible that the boy would have been aware of little difference as he continued under the watchful eye of Madame de Rambaud, preparing to occupy a throne that would never be his. Surely though, he recognized the anxiety in the adults around him, let alone the atmosphere that had descended over the palace that was now his whole world.

The little dauphin was with his family when they made their doomed escape to Varennes in June 1791, returning to even closer confinement once the escape plot was discovered. Stripped of his title by the new French Constitution, Louis was instead styled as Prince Royal but the real change in circumstances came on 10 August 1792 when a crowd stormed the palace and his beloved nurse fled in terror, never to see her charge again. Although Madame de Rambaud attempted to rejoin the family when they were imprisoned, her pleas fell on deaf ears and she remained separated from them for what remained of their lives.

As the terrified royal family gathered within the walls of the palace the situation seemed hopeless, their only chance of safety offered by the promise of refuge in the Legislative Assembly. Faced with the fury of the mob and flanked by columns of troops, the fearful procession made its journey to what they must have prayed was safety. Sanctuary was indeed offered but it carried a heavy cost and the family was whisked off to the Temple, to begin their lives as prisoners.

Here Louis and Marie Antoinette did what they could to keep their children amused and entertained. In the notorious Temple tower the family lived a simple yet not entirely unpleasant life, tended to by servants even as the catcalls rang in their ears from the crowds that gathered outside.

Although Louis XVI was executed on 21 January 1793, his son was never officially crowned king. Of course, those who supported the monarchy certainly regarded him as Sovereign and though plots were hatched to save the family and restore the throne, these never reached fruition. Instead, on 3 July 1793, Louis Charles was finally and permanently removed from what little family he still had left.

At the moment of separation Louis and Marie Antoinette fought fiercely to stay together. Overcome with terror the little boy clung to his hysterical mother with all his might yet it was to no end, for what could such a pair do against the forces of the government? When they were finally pulled apart the distraught twosome could not be comforted for days, with Marie Antoinette straining to catch a glimpse of her boy when he exercised, desperate to hear just a snatch of his voice.

The young king was placed in the care of cobbler Antoine Simon, and his wife, Marie-Jeanne, devoted followers of the Revolution. Reports began to circulate that Louis was a virtual slave, yet tales of abuse and unhappiness were never definitely proven. In fact, it would seem that Louis was not maltreated by the couple, though their language was earthy and they certainly disavowed the boy of any pretensions he might harbour towards one day being the king of France.

However, there are forms of abuse other than physical and at just 8-years-old, Louis was given enough alcohol to render him drunk, whilst the more he swore and entertained his carers and jailers, the more they seemed to approve. Like any child thrust into such a desperate situation, Louis craved this approval and did all he could to win it, perhaps grasping for any modicum of affection in the harsh new world that had become his reality.

Perhaps the worst abuse perpetrated against Louis was the cruel decision to record his signature on testimonies claiming that he was routinely sexually abused by his mother and other female members of his family. A hernia in his groin caused by a playtime accident was presented as evidence of abuse and Louis, desperate to please, would not recant his statement even when his sister begged him to do so.

When Marie-Jeanne Simon fell ill in January 1794, Louis was returned to the Temple and found himself in far harsher circumstances than he had known before. Now very definitely a prisoner, when politician Jean–Baptiste Harmand visited the little boy he was shocked to see the confinement in which the child was suffering. Physically debilitated, his body riddled with lice and sores, Louis was so frail he could barely stand and seemed unable or unwilling to communicate, eating little and moving less. He had no friends amongst his jailers, precious little human contact and no childish distractions from his lonely fate. It appeared as though, mindful that the execution of a child was a step too far, those who ruled had decided simply to let nature take its course; abandoned, uncared for and alone, Louis was simply being left to die.

Even when new carers were appointed and efforts made to clean his cell and offer him a modicum of comfort, Louis barely noticed. He regarded those around him with silent disinterest, spending his days huddled on his meagre bed in solitude. One's heart can only bleed for this child, torn from his family and all that was familiar and placed in an environment usually reserved for the worst criminals. He was, of course, unable to thrive in such conditions and his already frail health deteriorated at an alarming rate.

When the boy fell ill in May 1795 he was seen by a number of doctors, yet urgency did not seem to be the order of the day. Finally, on 8 June 1795, word was issued that Louis had died of tuberculosis in his cell, utterly alone in his final moments. He was buried in an unmarked grave two days later and, according to surgeon Philippe-Jean Pelletan, his frail body was scarred all over with the evidence of physical abuse. Before Louis was placed in his meagre resting place, Pelletan removed his heart and in 1795 it was placed in the Basilica of Saint-Denis, the little boy memorialized alongside his family.

Almost immediately, rumours began to circulate that Louis was not dead at all and that the child confined in that dark cell was not and never had been the little king. Stories soon spread that the young monarch had been smuggled to safety, and lived on in hiding but the rumours of Louis's death continued to be simply conjecture and it would seem that the little boy really *did* endure such a terrible life, his lonely fate one that nobody deserves, whether king or pauper.

'She would have been my friend'

Princess Sophie de France (Bourbon)
Versailles, France, 9 July 1786–Versailles, France, 19 June 1787

As anyone with a love of history knows, one of the saddest truths of delving into the past are the number of stories that end almost before they have started, with a whole lifetime's worth of experience packed into a few short, eventful years. In the Georgian era death was never too far away and if even the most robust of kings could be carried off by a sweet roll, then for a newborn baby the odds were stacked indeed.

The children of Louis XVI and Marie Antoinette were not, what with Revolution, exile and simple bad luck, the most fortunate of our monarchical broods and the short life story of Princess Sophie Hélène Béatrice is a tragedy indeed.

This most divisive of European royal couples were delighted to welcome their daughter to Versailles and named her in honour of Louis's late aunt, Sophie de France. From the very moment of her birth, the health of Princess Sophie was far from robust and though not a physically slight child by any means, as the scant months of her life passed, it became apparent that the infant *Fille de France* was suffering from what appeared to be tuberculosis.

The royal household was quick to react, yet against such terrible odds there was little doctors could do to battle the infection. In the last week of her life Sophie began to cut her first teeth and it seemed that this was the final straw for the unfortunate little girl. The dental pains caused Sophie to undergo violent and frightening convulsions and for the last few days of her tragically short life, she endured terrible suffering as her parents kept a constant vigil at her side.

The little princess died on 19 June 1787, her tiny body too weak to fight against the ailments that battered it. As her corpse lay in state awaiting burial, some attempted to calm the queen's distress by pointing out that one so young cannot have left much of a mark on the world. Marie Antoinette responded simply, 'She would have been my friend'.[7] The statement is devastating in its humanity, the words of a mother in anguish, not a queen in formal mourning.

Sophie's death left the king and queen utterly inconsolable yet fate had another cruel card to play. Just two years later, yet another child of the house of Bourbon would die a premature death, not to mention the tragic, terrible fate that awaited their son who would become a prisoner, dauphin and uncrowned king.

'My birth and my death; that is my whole story'

Napoleon II, Duke of Reichstadt (Bonaparte)

Paris, France, 20 March 1811–
Vienna, Austria, 22 July 1832

Not all the children we meet in this chapter led short lives and we won't be following them all to the grave. There was, of course, another man who bore the name Napoleon – a young man who died aged just 21 in the closing years of the Georgian era. Though the world would never be the same for his father's part in it, for the son who shared his name, life was over before it really had a chance to begin.

Napoleon was desperate for a son and heir to secure his succession, so much so that he was willing to divorce the love of his life, Joséphine, to marry another. The woman he chose was Marie Louise of Austria and the longed-for son was born just a year after that second marriage took place. As the boy lay in his cradle at the Tuileries Palace 101 cannons were fired to mark the occasion as cheers of jubilation rang out across the French capital

To the people of Paris, the continuing cannon fire meant just one thing: a boy had been born to the house of Bonaparte. Had the child been a girl, only twenty-one cannons would have fired and the racket saw much rejoicing among courtiers and public alike. Whilst some children might be given cuddly toys and rattles in the cradle, Napoleon II received all of that and more, including the titles of Prince Imperial and King of Rome. He was baptized at Notre Dame de Paris Cathedral by his father's uncle, Cardinal Joseph Fesch and his ceremonial, flamboyantly staged christening was witnessed by nobles and an enormous audience of Parisians who had gathered for the occasion. As the crowds pressed forward for the slightest glimpse of the newborn, the emperor lifted his son high above his head so that the people might see him, their cheers ringing in his ears.

Napoleon doted on his young namesake and the two spent hours together, with the little boy often playing beside his father whilst the emperor worked on affairs of state. When business was concluded, then father and son would indulge in rambunctious play, with Napoleon fond of affectionately pranking his young son or even starting the occasional food fight!

The childhood care of the sensitive, unassuming young man was overseen by Louise Charlotte Françoise Le Tellier de Montesquiou, the governess of the children of France. Under her tutelage, the boy flourished and the pair developed a strong and abiding bond. Madame de Montesquiou cared for him as though he was her own son, much to the occasional annoyance of Napoleon II's emotionally distant mother.

The little boy's early years were a tumultuous time in France as his father struggled to keep control of the First French Empire, which had never been more fractured. Even as he lost his grip on power, Napoleon visited his wife and three-year-old son on 24 January 1814 for a fateful goodbye; he could not know then that he would never see the boy nor Marie Louise again.

When Napoleon finally abdicated in April of 1814 he named his infant son as his successor. Of course, the government knew that the Empire was in its death throes, so the little boy was not acknowledged as emperor. In fact, all of this became academic when, days later, Napoleon was forced to give up his familial rights to the French throne, depriving his son of the right to rule forever. Despite this, the boy was known as Napoleon II, emperor in nothing but name.

Just prior to Napoleon's abdication and exile to Elba, mother and child left the Tuileries to travel to Rambouillet for a reunion with Marie Louise's father, Emperor Francis II of Austria. Here they did not linger and as news spread of the abdication, Marie Louise and her son departed France forever to begin their life anew in her native land of Austria. Despite a movement to put Napoleon II on the throne of France following his father's defeat at Waterloo, the new French Commission never called him to power and he continued to live his life in waiting.

Once the former emperor was exiled to St Helena, Marie Louise and her son made their home in the safety of Schönbrunn Palace in Vienna. Life was all luxury and privilege, yet the boy became a valuable political pawn at court and fell under the particular influence of Austrian Foreign Minister and later Chancellor, Prince Klemens von Metternich. A constant presence in the life of the child, Metternich saw the value in winning the boy's trust and used him as leverage in dealings between Austria and France.

The Congress of Vienna gave Marie Louise the title of Duchess of Parma, though when Marie Louise left for Parma in 1816, the little boy did not go with her. Instead, Napoleon II was left in the loving care of his grandfather and given the nickname, *Franz*.

Franz was told little of his father yet asked after him often and when he was informed of Napoleon's death, the boy, by now 10, was understandably distraught. With his mother hundreds of miles away and his father dead, Franz devoted himself to his studies under his tutor, Maurice Dietrichstein, and was an intelligent, lively child with a love of the outdoors. Dietrichstein wrote to Marie Louise often with reports of her son, charting his growth from a frivolous boy to a poised, ambitious young man who seemed able to charm all those who knew him. However, Franz and Dietrichstein disagreed on the younger man's desire to prove himself on the battlefield, an ambition that was continually denied him. Dietrichstein thought his charge emotionally immature and, perhaps surprisingly, the young man appeared to take his tutor's views on board, no doubt trusting the judgment of the man who had been his companion and protector for more than a decade.

Although he appeared to want for nothing, Franz continued to feel a deep sadness at his father's death and mother's absence and in 1832, Franz reached the final months of what had been a lonely life. Marie Louise finally returned to Austria and was at her son's side when he succumbed to tuberculosis, at 21. His last, poignant words were, 'My birth and my death; that is my whole story,'[8] a sad epitaph to the story of a life that never really had a chance to be lived.

Act Two

Marriage

'Marriage has many pains, but celibacy has no pleasures.'

Samuel Johnson, 1759

And so our jaunt through the courts brings us to the altar, as inevitably it must in a world ruled by marriage, heirs and spares. There was precious little room for love in the planning of a royal match in Georgian times, as territory, politics and the all-important need to propagate a line ruled supreme. Of course, it would be untrue to claim that there were *no* happy royal unions and some of the most successful were also the most unlikely.

Each country had its own particular wish list when it came to putting together a royal couple but in England things were made considerably more complicated by the 1772 introduction of the Royal Marriages Act. King George III created the Act as a dismayed response to his brother, Henry, Duke of Cumberland and Strathearn's 1771 marriage to a commoner, Mrs Anne Horton. Dismay would later turn to horror when George discovered the secret marriage of another brother, William Henry, Duke of Gloucester and Edinburgh, to Maria Walpole. Though the king did not know of this second marriage when the Act was enshrined in law, he believed that he could rest assured that such a scandalous love match would never happen again.

Oh, to be so naive.

The Act set down the stringent rules under which members of the royal family could marry; its intention being to protect the integrity of the royal household. Central to its power was the clause that all descendants of George II must secure the official consent of the reigning monarch before they were permitted to marry. The consent must be approved under the Great Seal (a seal used to symbolize the sovereign's approval) and registered by the Privy Council and, if this consent was not achieved, and these protocols not followed, the marriage was not considered legal.

The Act read as follows: 'That no descendant of the body of his late majesty King George the Second, male or female, (other than the issue of princesses who have married, or may hereafter marry, into foreign families) shall be capable of contracting matrimony without the previous consent of his Majesty, his heirs, or successors, signified under the great seal, and declared in council, (which consent, to preserve the memory thereof is hereby directed to be set out in the licence and register of marriage, and to be entered in the books of the privy council); and that every marriage, or matrimonial contract, of any such descendant, without such consent first had and obtained, shall be null and void, to all intents and purposes whatsoever.'

However, there was a small get-out for those over the age of 25, who, if refused permission to marry, could give notice of the intended wedding to the Privy Council. One year after that notice was given they would be allowed to marry, on condition that Parliament had not refused the match. In fact, this condition was not required as no request for consent was denied by the Sovereign.

As we will discover, there were already secret marriages in place that were rendered null and void by the Act. In some cases, the king allowed for these to be legitimized but in others, notably that of the scandalous Prince of Wales and Maria Fitzherbert, no official recognition of the marriage was requested. Of course, in this particular case, the groom refused to acknowledge that the wedding had actually taken place, so it was a somewhat moot point.

So let us travel from France to England and Russia and beyond for a look at arranged marriages that turned to devotion, love matches that ended in tragedy and more besides. Some of these players will make later appearances in our gallop through royal scandals, because life in the courts of Europe was never predictable.

'I will not marry the pig snout!'

Sophia Dorothea of Celle and George I (Hanover)

22 November 1682, Celle, Germany

This is the tale of the man who would one day wear the crown as George I and the woman he married – the very founders of the Georgian era. It is a tale of a marriage gone horribly wrong. If George III was to be a devoted husband and George II an errant one, then the first Georgian king set the bar for the marital catastrophe that the notorious George IV would fuel afresh more than a century later.

As was the case for George IV and Caroline of Brunswick, the reason behind George I's marriage to his cousin, Sophia Dorothea of Celle, had little to do with love. Instead, it was a match made entirely for financial and territorial convenience, as so many have been throughout royal history. Of course, any number of other noble marriages began in such circumstances but it is fair to say that this one turned out to be nastier than most.

A marriage in which the groom's mother takes a dislike to her future daughter-in-law and goes out of her way to keep herself as the number one woman in her son's life, is not that uncommon. Unpleasant though this experience must be for the bride concerned, if the match is one of affection then this unfortunate obstacle might well be overcome. However, when even the groom isn't quite sold on the marriage let alone the woman he is about to take as a wife, it is a problem that is likely to get worse. So it was with Sophia, the future Electress of Hanover and her son, George.

There was no denying that a marriage between Sophia Dorothea and George would be of enormous financial advantage and would cement powerful ties between Celle and Hanover, yet George's mother was not happy with the match.

The mother of the bride, far from being a woman of impeccable credentials, was the polar opposite of what Sophia thought of as *ideal*. In fact, Éléonore Desmier d'Olbreuse was a Huguenot of noble but not *royal* birth and her marriage to Sophia Dorothea's father, George William, Duke of Brunswick-Lüneburg, had been morganatic: meaning they were from different social ranks, and Sophia Dorothea's father was prohibited from passing on his title or privileges to his wife or children. Sophia Dorothea's legitimacy at birth had been questionable at best and though the couple were later officially married and their daughter legitimized, it was hardly the perfect start in life for a future queen.

The future Electress of Hanover regarded her potential daughter-in-law just a little sniffily, not entirely convinced that this girl was an adequate wife for the future elector. However, money can be a tremendous leveller, and she eventually decided that, given the inarguable financial and territorial benefits of the union, she would withdraw her complaints and let the marriage go ahead.

If the groom's family was uncertain then Sophia Dorothea herself was horrified and upon being told of the betrothal declared: 'I will not marry the pig snout!',[9] dashing George's miniature against the wall. It was a spirited but pointless tantrum yet George was left in no doubt as to her feelings when, upon their first meeting, Sophia Dorothea became so overwhelmed with misery that she fainted clean away. This was an inauspicious start to a miserable married life and when the wedding took place on 22 November 1682, we can only imagine what both parties must have been thinking.

Still they managed to put their differences aside for a few minutes at least because, less than twelve months after they were married, Sophia Dorothea gave birth to a son. The baby, a boy named George Augustus, would become better known to history as King George II. That they had one child is remarkable given their dislike for each other, but perhaps more surprising is the fact that, five years after the wedding, Sophia bore George a daughter, also named Sophia Dorothea.

However, something clearly went badly wrong in the relationship between the man who would be George I and his wife who would, had things run smoothly, become the first Georgian queen. What, then, were the circumstances that led to the dissolution of the marriage of the Electoral Prince and Princess of Hanover?

There were *two* women at George's side when he arrived in England to take the throne. One was his illegitimate half-sister, Sophia von Kielmansegg, who was nicknamed *the Elephant,* and the second was Melusine von der Schulenberg, better known to the people of England as *the Maypole,* among other less complimentary things. Later the Duchess of Kendal, she was with George when he died, but the one thing she never became, no matter what she may have wanted, was his wife. Melusine was a Maid of Honour to George's mother, and she and George had a long and loving relationship, resulting in the birth of three children in 1692, 1693 and 1701, all of whom were obviously exempt from succession. He made no effort to keep this liaison a secret from his wife and when she challenged him about it, George physically attacked Sophia Dorothea. It was a pivotal moment in the royal marriage because Princess Sophia then embarked on an affair of her own.

For her confidante, the Electoral Princess chose Count Philip Christoph von Königsmarck, a Swedish soldier whom she had first met when they were in their teens. Following the example of her husband, Sophia Dorothea made no secret of her friendship with the count and by 1689 the Hanoverian court was alive with gossip about the pair. Following a second altercation in which George attempted to strangle his wife when she confronted him about his affair, Sophia Dorothea hatched a plot to flee Hanover and the man she had come to despise. It was an audacious and scandalous plan but one can hardly judge the electoral princess, who had perhaps reached the final straw when her husband's hands were locked around her throat.

The couple decided to head for Wolfenbüttel but their scheme was doomed to fail and in July 1694, following a liaison with Sophia Dorothea, Count von Königsmarck simply disappeared, never to be seen again. In *Memoirs of Sophia Dorothea, Consort of George I*, the murder of the count is attributed to drunken courtiers, his corpse concealed beneath quicklime, whilst historian and Whig politician Horace Walpole suggested that he was strangled, his body hidden beneath the floorboards of the Leineschloss. To add spice to an already unpleasant scandal, one name that has been consistently implicated in the disappearance is that of Countess Clara Elisabeth Von Platen, a lady of influence thanks to her *intimate* friendship with George's father.

The countess was also rumoured to be a lover of von Königsmarck and was known for a fiery and volatile temper. Was Clara the woman who blew the whistle on the lovers and engineered a murder to save the royal face or was it a moment of madness from loyal courtiers? We will never know for sure, and the victim and killers took the secret to their respective graves if, indeed, von Königsmarck even *had* a grave to call his own.

One thing that all appear to agree on is that the count was murdered, but who was behind the plot and what became of the body remains a mystery. Some say he was thrown into the river Leine, others that his dismembered body never left the castle at all yet, whatever the lost truth, he was never seen again. We cannot know if George himself was involved; perhaps the conspiracy was headed by his parents or was even the work of overly-zealous courtiers who simply took it upon themselves to rid Hanover of a potential embarrassment, the 'turbulent priest' of George's marriage. Whatever the truth of the matter, the damage was done.

On the day of von Königsmarck's disappearance, Sophia Dorothea was confined to her rooms as her husband, father and father-in-law discussed what they should do with this troublesome woman. Eventually they decided that the quickest and cleanest route was to have the marriage dissolved and this was done in December 1694. The reason for the dissolution was not adultery; instead, it was claimed that Sophia Dorothea had abandoned her husband who, let us not forget, had beaten, throttled and humiliated her.

Even now though, Sophia Dorothea would not be allowed the escape she longed for and, still only in her late twenties, the unfortunate woman was imprisoned in Germany's Ahlden House. She was attended to by a retinue of staff, all of whom were charged with reporting on her behaviour to Hanover, and here she would remain in lonely seclusion.

Although the circumstances of Sophia Dorothea's imprisonment were not physically unpleasant, even the most comfortable cell is still a prison and she was denied all access to her children whilst her father did not visit her either. Her son, later to be George II, never forgave his father for this forced, unforgiving separation from his mother, and it was a major source of the animosity between the pair in the turbulent years to come.

Sophia Dorothea never left her gilded cage and died in the castle after three decades of confinement, no doubt ruing the day that she married 'the pig snout' who treated her so badly.

The Mysterious Monsieur de Busch

Caroline of Ansbach and George II (Hohenzollern, Hanover)

2 September 1705, Hanover, Germany

Perhaps unsurprisingly, given the catalogue of adultery, abuse and imprisonment that George I inflicted on Sophia Dorothea, their son, the man who would one day be George II did not always see eye to eye with his father. The enforced separation of the young man and his mother never left George and if tales of him swimming the moat of Sophia Dorothea's prison in an effort to find her are somewhat spurious, we can hardly doubt that such a sudden separation must have had a traumatic and long-lasting impact on a boy who was not even in his teens.

All too keenly aware of how disastrously his own union had turned out, the elector and future king was convinced that his son should have a shot at a happier match. Therefore, he decided, the groom to be must at least meet his bride to be before the announcement was made, lest there be a repeat of the unfortunate 'pig snout' incident that had greeted his own engagement. The lady in question was Princess Caroline of Ansbach, an orphaned girl who had caught the appraising eye of Dowager Electress Sophia of Hanover, George's grandmother. The dowager was immensely impressed by the young lady's intelligence and good nature and surmised that, if her grandson did not act fast, he would lose this most attractive proposition. Act fast he did, and the couple's first meeting was like something from a fairytale as young George, his identity concealed, made the trip to meet his prospective intended.

In the summer of 1705, a well-mannered, cultured gentleman named Monsieur de Busch arrived at Triesdorf to spend the summer at the Ansbach court. In true romantic style, the dashing *Monsieur de Busch* was none other than the young Prince George in disguise and upon meeting Caroline, he found himself utterly bewitched by the young woman's beauty and character. We cannot know whether she saw through the prince's act but once the official approach was made and her guardian accepted the proposal, Caroline was utterly delighted.

The eager bride and her equally keen groom were married on 2 September 1705 in Hanover before they took up residence in the Leineschloss, where Caroline continued to enchant all who knew her. She eventually bore her husband nine children but this marriage, with its fairytale beginnings, was not without its *very* rocky patches. Still, time and again they returned to one another's arms and Caroline remained one of her husband's most valued advisers; she was even entrusted with the kingdom itself, serving as regent during George's absences.

When Caroline fell ill with smallpox, George set aside his mistresses to take his devoted place at her bedside and their marriage could not have been more different to the unhappy experience of George I and his unfortunate wife. It was a partnership that endured for decades, all thanks to a clandestine trip by the mysterious *Monsieur de Busch*.

The Teenage Widow

Louise Élisabeth d'Orléans and Louis I (Bourbon)

20 January 1722, Lerma, Spain

To our modern sensibilities, the idea that a girl of just 11 years old might be taken from her family to another country and married to a boy barely two years her senior is utterly unconscionable, yet for the daughter of the Regent of France, Philippe II, and Françoise Marie de Bourbon, that is precisely how childhood came to a shuddering, final halt. Some young ladies, such as Marie Antoinette and her sisters, were raised with the intention of making high profile marriages, but the woefully underprepared Louise Élisabeth was not one of these. Instead, she was thrust into the spotlight by political manoeuvrings far beyond her control.

Mademoiselle de Montpensier, as the girl was known, lived her early life with the Benedictine sisters at Saint Paul, her existence a solitary one. As the fourth of six daughters, Louise Élisabeth did not see much of her parents, yet had they foreseen the fate that awaited her, no doubt the disinterested duke and duchess would have committed a little more to her education. Instead she was left to her own devices and was barely taught how to behave in *private*, and was in no way prepared for the minefield of court life.

By the time she was in double figures Louise Élisabeth was a badly-behaved, hot-tempered young lady. Her manners were not so much lacking as non-existent, hardly making her the ideal candidate for the strict Spanish court where she was to end up. However, her family had reckoned without the War of the Quadruple Alliance and when it broke out, good manners and upbringing were second to the future of the houses of Europe.

Needing to cement alliances at all costs to ensure they were not swept away by the war, Philip V of Spain and Philippe II of France negotiated a fragile peace, at the core of which lay a number of marriages between the Spanish and French Bourbon courts. In the event, the only one of these betrothals to actually come to fruition was that of Louise Élisabeth and Louis, Prince of Asturias, heir to the Spanish throne. Perhaps unsurprisingly, given the disposition of the bride and the rather rushed plans for the betrothal, it was an unmitigated disaster.

In a particularly stinging irony, one of the ultimately abandoned marriages included in the initial negotiations between France and Spain was that of Louise Élisabeth's sister, Philippine Élisabeth and the future Charles III of Spain. Political machinations put paid to this particular union yet it was the only proposed marriage amongst those under discussion that might actually have been a success. Unlike so many of their contemporaries, Charles and Philippine fell in love almost at first sight and when their marriage was indefinitely postponed, they strove without success to secure their union. If only that were the case for the unfortunate Louise Élisabeth, whose fate was sealed despite her wishes to the contrary.

Immediately following the proxy marriage the bride left for Madrid carrying an enormous dowry of four million livres. She was handed over to the Spanish on the Île des Faisans and from there travelled on to Lerma where her new family awaited, little suspecting the unhappy and ill-tempered young bride who was about to land at court.

The wedding ceremony on 20 January 1722 was followed by an enormous celebration, culminating in a ball. At the close of festivities, according to tradition, the newlyweds were followed to their bedchamber by the entire court. As the courtiers watched, the young couple settled in bed together and the curtains were ceremoniously drawn, signalling an end to the celebration and the forthcoming consummation of the new royal marriage.

In fact, Louis left the bedroom almost as soon as the courtiers retired and as the celebratory atmosphere of the wedding began to fade, the new Princess of Asturias found that she was far from welcome in her adopted homeland. In the austere Spanish court her earthy manners and lack of education did not sit well and she was mocked. As her husband preferred his own company and was often absent, Louise Élisabeth found herself friendless and isolated in this strange new world. The final straw came when she refused to attend a ball given in her honour by her stepmother-in-law, Elisabeth Farnese. Though the queen had done her best to bridge the distance between her stepson and his bride, she now threw her hands up in despair, washing them of this ill-mannered young princess.

Although Louis succeeded to the throne in January 1724, upon his father's abdication, his reign was a short one and he succumbed to smallpox in August of that same year. Widowed and isolated at just 14, the Spanish court took one look at Louise Élisabeth and decided that she was the last person they wanted hanging around. Understandably, when it was suggested that the widow might prefer to return to France she put up no resistance. In fact, her agreement was most fortuitous for the French as it gave them a very handy way to break off the engagement of Louis XV and the Infanta Mariana Victoria of Spain, as we will see very shortly.

With Louise Élisabeth just a memory, Philip V, newly returned to the throne, moved to have the childless marriage annulled. It was an unhappy end to a disastrous match and one that should have served as a salutary lesson for just how badly arranged unions could go.

Of course, it did no such thing…

Farewell to the Infanta

Marie Leszczyńska and Louis XV (Leszczyński, Bourbon)

5 September 1725, Fontainebleau, France

If the wheeler-dealer world of royal marriages was something akin to a very luxurious, very cynical marketplace, then like any salesperson, the houses of Europe never knowingly undersold their choicest goods. As in any business, some things were considered that little bit more prestigious than others and the house of Bourbon knew all too well the value of their own marital prospects. Power, territory, wealth and prestige were all theirs to command and any son or daughter of the French ruling family would be a valuable prize to those sometimes not *quite* so influential families that looked on hungrily across the borders of the continent.

Of all the bachelors on the monarchical marriage market, 11-year-old Louis XV was undoubtedly one of the most sought after and in 1721, the Bourbon court was searching for a suitable bride. Looking back from three centuries distance the idea of an 11-year-old being married is difficult to stomach but for our eighteenth century royals, it was nothing but business. Securing a royal marriage and with it all the territorial, financial and other gains that could be negotiated was vital and like all big plans, the sooner the match could be concluded, the better.

When the War of the Quadruple Alliance came to an end in 1720 it left relations between France and Spain on a knife edge. Not surprisingly, since one of Spain's ambitions for the war had been to capture the French throne.

As the two powers looked to one another with suspicion, their respective governments decided that the easiest way to ensure no future flare ups was to forge bonds that began at the altar and led all the way to the marriage bed. Tense discussions began and with all the care of a cartographer at their craft, a web of intricate dynastic marriages was woven. The jewel in the crown of this nuptial network was the announcement of the engagement of Louis XV to his cousin, the Infanta Mariana Victoria of Spain who, at eight years his junior, was to be a bride before the concept could mean anything to her.

The French ambassador, Louis de Rouvroy, Duke of Saint-Simon, officially made the proposal on 25 November 1721 and it was accepted with much formality and ceremony. With the deal done, Mariana was brought from Spain and installed at the Palais du Louvre in the care of Marie Anne de Bourbon. Here she would be raised as a member of the Bourbon court and schooled in French manners and etiquette until she was ready to marry. In fact, the charming little girl proved herself wildly popular, enchanting courtiers with her intelligence and character, her childish enthusiasm infectious. Indeed, the only person who *didn't* seem enthralled by the little Infanta was her intended husband who, perhaps unsurprisingly for a boy on the cusp of adolescence, had no interest whatsoever in marriage and certainly not in the girl who was intended to be his bride.

There was, however, one other person who was less than enchanted with the little girl and he was determined to do something about it. Ambitious to a fault and as cunning as he was career-minded, French Prime Minister Louis Henri, Duke of Bourbon, looked on as young Louis endured health scare after health scare. Each one threatened to plunge the house of Bourbon into a succession crisis so he set to scheming, and eventually managed to usurp the infanta's clam to her fiancé in a fairly dazzling bit of political manoeuvring. In some ways it's difficult to fault his common sense as there was no guaranteed Bourbon heir in place should the boy die and, with the bride to be no more than a child herself, even a swift marriage could not possibly result in the quick production of an heir. Instead, should the worst happen and Louis die, then the house of Orléans would press its long-nursed claim to the French throne and this, the prime minister decided, would *never* do.

Like any loyal advisor, the duke assured the king that he only had the best interests of the crown at heart. Still, he mused, might it be wise to think about taking an older bride and getting on with the business in hand, to put it delicately? Accordingly, the prime minister presented the adolescent Louis with what must have been a mind-boggling list of ninety-nine possible alternative brides. Cannily included on the list were two of the duke's own sisters and, crucially, all of the prospective brides were already of child-bearing age.

All of this politicking rather ignored the fact that the king was already betrothed and regardless of the wishes of the prime minister, any attempt to break the engagement could be disastrous. However, fate was on the side of the ambitious politician and no doubt he and the court heaved a collective sigh of relief in 1724 when bad – or good, if you were French – news reached them from Spain with reports of Louis I's death at the age of just 17.

The death of the Spanish monarch left his unhappy, unsettled and unpopular widow, Louise Élisabeth d'Orléans, at something of a loose end. Childless and without friends, she simply didn't fit in at her adopted court which was desperate to send her home to France and wash its hands of a marriage that had been disastrous from the beginning. It was the perfect opportunity and the French seized it, negotiating what was considered to be a fair exchange. The engagement would be broken and the little infanta returned to Madrid, whilst Élisabeth would return to her French homeland. The rejected infanta eventually bagged herself another monarch in the shape of Joseph I of Portugal but the political ramifications of the broken engagement would ring on for years and, as Mariana Victoria readjusted to life in her homeland, in France the marriage negotiations rumbled on.

The prime minister's list now became more important than ever yet one by one the politicians and court considered and discounted the suggested candidates. For every likely bride there was opposition, for every favoured young lady a rebuttal, yet one name kept coming up again and again. That name belonged to something of an outsider although, one might ungenerously say, it was also something of a safe bet.

At twenty-one, Marie Leszczyńska was not the prettiest or the most powerful and far from the most wealthy, but she was, all began to murmur, the most uncontroversial. This daughter of a deposed Polish king would bring with her no intrigue nor any possibility of future war and calamity; indeed, she would provide nothing but an uncomplicated marital match.

Once again negotiations began but this time, they would be over quickly and to the delight of all political parties involved. In order to ensure that no unexpected problems might arise and sour the scheme, on 15 August 1725, Marie and Louis were married by proxy, the list of ninety nine finally whittled down to one *lucky* girl. The next thing was to get husband and wife in a room together and let the business of producing heirs begin, so Marie took to the road and the first chapter of her new life.

The bride arrived at the Château de Fontainebleau on 4 September. Here she was introduced to her illustrious husband and the following day, the couple were formally married. At first, the bride and groom seemed to delight in one another's company, but sadly, this unexpected happiness was not to last.

Even as the French people took their new queen to their hearts, the notoriously cliquey Bourbon court soon decided that Marie was not to their liking at all. For a start, she was poor and on top of that, plain. Taken alone or even in tandem these obstacles were not insurmountable should she prove at least to be fertile… but was she?

Perhaps not, the court realized, as month after month went by without any happy announcement.

The heir seemed to take forever to appear but eventually appear he did and though Marie bore her husband ten children, the couple's initial happiness eventually dwindled away. Following one final traumatic pregnancy the queen withdrew from the marital bed leaving the king to take solace in the arms of his mistresses. Among them was a lady whose fame would eventually eclipse that of his wife, a certain Madame de Pompadour, an icon of Versailles.

The Night Emperor

Elizabeth of Russia and Alexei Razumovsky (Romanov)

1742, Perovo, Russia

One might be forgiven for thinking that it was always male royals who made wildly unsuitable matches, falling for women their parents disapproved of, installing them as wives in all but name or even, now and again, marrying them and dealing with the consequences later. Of course, there were plenty of ladies who threw caution to the wind too and the house of Romanov knew one or two controversies of its own. One such scandal is a tale of rags to riches that would not be out of place in the golden age of Hollywood, albeit a golden age that was happy to tell a story of imprisoned children driven to an early grave and multiple palace coups. It even comes with a ready-made title that would look good on any billboard, *The Night Emperor*.

The story began far from St Petersburg on a Cossack farm in the Ukrainian village of Lemeshi, where a boy named Oleksiy Rozum was born in 1709. Although he would one day go by the far grander name of Count Alexei Razumovsky, the child who was born into abject poverty could only dream of a different life, as he toiled from dawn to dusk to earn a meagre living as a shepherd.

Remarkably Razumovsky had a gift for music, having the most amazing voice. When he sang in the local church choir he could forget his cares and for those precious minutes, be something more than a peasant shepherd. Life had a most pleasant surprise in store for Razumovsky though, and his whole future changed in a twist of fate which brought a Russian colonel named Vyshnevsky to Lemeshi in 1731, searching for a place where he might spend the night.

Vyshnevsky was on his way back to Russia from a trip to Hungary, accompanying a shipment of wine that was intended for Empress Anna. No doubt the colonel had little in mind other than a good night's rest and a safe return home yet when he went to worship in the village, the sound of Razumovsky's outstanding voice shook him wide awake. The colonel knew that the empress would be equally enamoured at the young man's talent and invited Razumovsky to return to Russia with him. Of course, a new life at the Romanov court was an opportunity that the young shepherd was hardly going to turn down and Razumovsky accepted without hesitation, leaving poverty behind him forever.

In Moscow, Elizabeth Petrovna, the 22-year-old daughter of Peter the Great and Catherine I, was living an unfulfilled life at court. The beautiful young woman had fallen from favour thanks to internal politics and now sought solace and fun in a series of unsuitable relationships with men who were far from her social equal, each one more doomed to failure than the last. None of these men would make a suitable marriage for the girl who held a legitimate claim to the throne of Russia and her cousin, Empress Anna, was determined to marry her off as a matter of urgency, hopefully to a husband who lived far from the centre of power. Things wouldn't quite play out that way, of course, and as an unfortunate young man named Ivan was to discover elsewhere in this book, Elizabeth had plenty of cunning of her own.

Needless to say, when Elizabeth and Razumovsky met in St Petersburg, the young lady with a taste for servants and coachmen fell for more than his voice and the pair began a heated affair. Her own mother had started life as a peasant so Elizabeth knew all too well that love and marriage could overcome the boundaries of social class and wealth if one had the tenacity and passion to see it through. Razumovsky rose swiftly through the ranks of the court thanks to his attachment to Elizabeth and as no suitable marriage match appeared for the young woman, their affection grew deeper still.

A year after the empress died in 1740, Elizabeth instigated a coup that deposed the regent, Anna Leopoldovna, and eventually placed the infant Ivan VI in prison. Whilst Ivan's fate was one of the saddest in the eighteenth century courts, for Razumovsky things could not have been better. He was no longer simply the lover of the daughter of Peter the Great, but the consort of the Empress and Autocrat of All the Russias, a position of unimaginable influence. So open were the couple about their relationship that Razumovsky acquired the nickname, *the Night Emperor*, thanks to his unapologetic assignations in Elizabeth's bedchamber.

Deeply in love with the man who stood alongside her during the coup that began her two decade reign, Elizabeth repaid Razumovsky richly. The Ukrainian shepherd and chorister was showered with titles and wealth yet the empress had one last honour to bestow on him; her hand in marriage.

Although no proof exists to support the marriage now, it is likely that the couple were united in a humble church in Perovo, near Moscow, in 1742. When rumours of the secret wedding leaked out at court, it came as a shock to nobody, that the *Night Emperor* had been legitimized at last. Razumovsky's benign influence was clear in Elizabeth's love of all things Ukrainian and her husband's family were no longer poor farmers, but living very well thanks to his connections. Indeed, some close relatives were even given office under Elizabeth's reign, demonstrating the trust she placed in her husband's counsel.

The couple's marriage lasted until Elizabeth died in 1762 when Razumovsky retreated into a quiet retirement, living out his remaining years in peaceful contentment, a long, long way from that farm in Lemeshi. No doubt he looked back on those early years and counted his blessings, especially the fateful day Colonel Vyshnevsky came to a humble church to hear the choir sing.

A Quiet Couple

Charlotte of Mecklenburg-Strelitz and George III (Mecklenburg-Strelitz, Hanover)

8 September 1761, London, England

A king without an heir is always a matter for concern but a king without so much as a queen is far worse. After all, with no bride, there is not even the faint hope of solving your succession woes. Of course, not having a wife was no bar to having children but they could never take the throne.

One such queenless king was George III, who ascended to the throne on 25 October 1760. Ill health and mental frailty would combine to ensure that George's future was anything but uneventful, yet for now there was no reason to worry about anything other than his lack of a bride. George was not without admirers, of course, and he admired them in turn but the royal marriage bed remained resolutely empty. A hopeful romance with Lady Sarah Lennox had dwindled to nothing as, looking to cement dynastic ties and ensure a smooth and uneventful future, Parliament lobbied hard for a German, Protestant bride. Throughout his life, George was never a man to make a fuss and he obligingly ended his liaison with Lady Lennox despite the mutual attraction. No doubt the lady was disappointed but with admirable fortitude she later agreed to serve as bridesmaid at the wedding where she had once dreamt of being the bride.

Just as a list of likely brides was presented at Versailles in 1725 and countless other royal houses throughout the centuries, so Parliament began to think about possible wives for the king. The long list was drawn up, discussed and whittled down until it could finally be provided to George. Misty-eyed for his beloved Sarah and full of swooning and longing he found fault with each and every one of the candidates. With a sigh, the politicians went back to the drawing board and assembled a second shortlist, no doubt with much complaining and fevered mopping of brows.

One of the names on the new list was that of Princess Sophia Charlotte of Mecklenburg-Strelitz who was six years younger than George and, crucially, utterly uncontroversial. Her family was respectable if not particularly illustrious and her youth made her the ideal candidate in the eyes of George's mother, Augusta of Saxe-Gotha, who did not want anyone *too* remarkable, lest her own influence be usurped. Intelligent, pretty, and with her only vices apparently a love of snuff and jewels, everyone agreed that Sophia Charlotte might well be the ideal candidate. There was the small matter of her being unable to speak English and only a little French but, if this was the only obstacle, it was hardly the worst thing one might imagine.

Charlotte's widowed mother, Elisabeth, negotiated the match and she did so with aplomb, smoothing the road for her daughter's forthcoming marriage. Sadly, Elisabeth would not live to see Charlotte marry and died in June 1761, just prior to the future queen's departure for England. Even with her entourage to accompany her, to make a trip to a new land whilst grieving for her mother must have put an enormous strain on the young bride. She maintained her composure admirably but behind her placid exterior, Charlotte mourned her lost mother keenly.

On the rough sea journey Charlotte utterly charmed her escorts whilst in England, George waited for his bride with undisguised enthusiasm, keen to meet the woman who appeared, on paper, to be just what he was looking for. Buoyed on by pleasing reports of the princess from those who had met her, he seemed to have finally set aside his adoration of Lady Sarah, the impending appearance of Charlotte proving quite a thrilling prospect. Upon her arrival at St James's Palace on 8 September 1761, 'the heartful regard of the King was particularly manifest'[10] and Charlotte threw herself at his feet in supplication, head bowed in deference. The king, gentleman that he was, helped his anxious bride to her feet and gently escorted her into the palace to meet his family.

The couple were married by Thomas Secker, Archbishop of Canterbury and from the very beginning, they seemed devoted to one another. This would set the store for the fifty -seven year marriage that was to follow, their love persisting through thick and thin. For George III there were to be no mistresses, official or otherwise; it seemed that, in Charlotte, he had truly found his soul mate.

George presented Charlotte with a diamond ring to be worn alongside her wedding ring; inscribed within the band was *Sept 8th 1761*. Charlotte appears to have been particularly touched by the ring and wore it from the day of her wedding to the day of her death.

Two weeks after the wedding the king and queen attended their Westminster Abbey coronation. With their shared dislike of being in the limelight, Charlotte and George did not particularly enjoy the ceremony and preferred to spend their time in contented seclusion. Certainly, they were secluded often enough to have fifteen children!

As the years passed and George began to succumb to the mental illness that would later dominate him, Charlotte's devotion never lessened, She bore the exhausting toll of caring for her husband with fortitude, turning to her unmarried daughters for company, needing someone to show her the affection that her ill husband became increasingly unable to demonstrate. The king and queen's marriage ended with Charlotte's death in 1818 and the king, his sanity gone, never knew that the wife he had once adored was dead, laid to rest in the castle that had become his home and hospital.

A Scandalous Walpole Bride

Maria Walpole and Prince William Henry, Duke of Gloucester and Edinburgh (Hanover)

6 September 1766, London, England

When George III heard that his brother, Prince Henry, Duke of Cumberland and Strathearn, had married the widowed commoner, Mrs Anne Horton, in 1771, he was incensed. What he didn't know was that yet another brother, Prince William Henry, Duke of Gloucester, had undertaken a secret marriage of his own years before Henry and Anne tied the knot. Of course, the truth could not remain hidden forever and when it came out, the relationship between the siblings was destroyed by this apparent deceit. Refreshingly though, this union was not a marriage of politics or dynasty building, or of territory and riches. Instead, this particular marriage came about for the rather simple reason that the bride and groom adored one another and wanted nothing more than to be together.

The name Walpole is one that casts a long shadow over the Georgian era, where it remains intrinsically linked with the formidable and divisive political giant, Robert Walpole. Robert was Maria's grandfather and in the eighteenth century, Walpole was a name that carried weight. One might imagine that the granddaughter of an illustrious character such as Walpole might be one social step up from some of the ladies who would later prove so popular with the house of Hanover, but despite her famous moniker, Maria was *not* from the most acceptable of beginnings.

In fact, Maria was the illegitimate daughter of unmarried politician, Edward Walpole, and his long-term mistress, Dorothy Clement. Although the devoted couple raised their children as though they were legitimate, the fact that Maria's parents never married was no secret in the gossipy hothouse of Georgian society. As Maria grew into a beautiful and cultured young woman, she was forever marked by the stigma of illegitimacy but thanks to her well-connected family, she was presented at court in 1758. She was an immediate hit with any number of starry-eyed young gents and soon found herself fending off a flurry of keen suitors, all of whom hoped to win the hand of the stunning young woman.

Illegitimate or not, when Maria was 22, she married a man twice her age, James, 2nd Earl Waldegrave, and together the couple had three children. Widowed after just four years, the rather more grandly titled Countess Waldegrave was still a beautiful young woman with her life ahead of her.

Sadly for Maria, beauty, title and elegance couldn't pay the bills and she was soon on the lookout for a new husband to keep her family in the style to which they had become accustomed. When William Cavendish-Bentinck, Duke of Portland, offered Maria his hand in marriage it seemed as though her future was set, yet to the astonishment of society, she turned him down. Why, the chattering classes wondered, would she make such an odd decision? What could possibly drive a woman to reject the proposal of the Duke of

Portland who offered a life few could even dream of? The reason was simple of course; Maria, Countess Waldegrave, was deeply in love with another.

On 6 September 1766, Maria married the object of her affection, Prince William Henry, Duke of Gloucester and Edinburgh, in a secret ceremony at her London home in Pall Mall. The wedding was officiated by a Doctor Morton and all involved were sworn to secrecy lest the duke's brother, George III, discover what had happened. As an illegitimate child and a widow, Maria was far from the ideal choice of royal bride and William correctly guessed that news of the relationship would horrify George, who put the dignity of his name and family above all else. To make matters worse, when Henry admitted his own marriage to Anne Horton in 1771 the king was enraged, banishing the couple and bringing in the Royal Marriages Act that would, he hoped, forever prevent another such upset.

One can only imagine the panic this must have sent through the Gloucester household; after all, what were they to do for the best? Should they admit their marriage and run the risk of having it declared illegal or keep quiet and hope for the best? Although rumours of the secret wedding reached George he dismissed them, sure that William would not lie to him as Henry had. Mindful of the affair between Maria and William, however, George was sure to find plenty of business for his brother to undertake in an effort to keep him from the company of his lover. If he hoped this would end talk of weddings once and for all he was, of course, far too late.

In the end, the decision was made for them when Maria fell pregnant with the first of three children and the couple came clean for the sake of the unborn child. To learn that another brother had also married a woman of lower rank was a step too far for the king, who reacted with utter fury. Although their marriage was eventually declared legal Maria and William were banished from court, not that either seems to have been particularly bothered. Instead the little family returned to their contented life at Gloucester Lodge, taking the occasional jaunt to Europe when debts demanded a fast escape from English shores.

Regardless of Marriage Acts and sibling fury, Maria and William's marriage was a happy one for many years and the brothers did eventually reconcile, though George never warmed to his sister-in-law. Sadly, for a match that seemed so perfect, as the years passed the couple began to slowly drift apart. Though Maria and William continued to live together, the affection between them cooled considerably and William found a new fancy in Lady Almeria Carpenter, Maria's lady-in-waiting and the eventual mother to his illegitimate daughter.

When William died in 1805, Maria lived on in respectable seclusion, caring for her children and involving herself ever more deeply in her passion for politics. She outlived the duke by just two years, the woman who had been born into scandal dying much-mourned and loved at the age of seventy-one.

Dentists and Dauphines

Marie Antoinette and Louis XVI (Habsburg-Lorraine, Bourbon)

16 May 1770, Versailles, France

Far from the fairytale romances of princesses and their Prince Charmings that fill the storybooks of old, love was very rarely a major ingredient in the marriages of our eighteenth century royal couples. Ruling a country was a matter of empire building, dynastic wrangling and keeping one step ahead or at least on the best side of your diplomatic rivals, and marriage was an invaluable tool for achieving such ends. A good marriage was not necessarily one in which mutual adoration was the key factor but one that could cement territorial claims or alliances, unite warring families and, of course, ensure the succession of the family on the throne.

Still, regardless of the motivations behind them, certain royal pairings have become iconic. Starting in youth and ending in tragedy, one such marriage must be the ill-fated union of a young Austrian archduchess and the heir to the throne of France. A gift to writers, filmmakers, artists and romantics everywhere, history remembers this unhappy couple as Marie Antoinette and Louis XVI, so let us see how the match of these ill-fated monarchs came to be.

The first moves in the game of royal marriage were made when Francis I, Holy Roman Emperor, died in 1765. His widow, Maria Theresa, had ruled alongside her husband for many years and continued to enjoy enormous influence once he was succeeded by their son, Joseph II. Though supposedly co-rulers there was no question that anyone other than Maria Theresa wielded power; shrewd and pragmatic, she was under no illusions about the importance of a good marriage and like a general planning a military campaign, she set to work on an intricate programme of dynastic unions. Maria Theresa envisioned a glittering future in which the Holy Roman Empire flourished at the altars of Europe, sowing its seeds across the continent, strengthening Austrian power and cementing valuable alliances.

Chief among Maria Theresa's targets was, of course, France. Thanks to the Seven Years' War, the alliance between the two countries had never been more fragile and she quite rightly determined that if she could hook a dauphin, then relations would improve exponentially. With a practiced eye the empress looked over the candidates available in her own house of Habsburg and found them, no doubt to her annoyance, wanting.

Some of her daughters were already betrothed, another was wed and still more were considered poor candidates thanks to ill health or the ravages of childhood smallpox. There was, however, her youngest daughter left who looked to be if not perfect, then at least a possible bride for the Dauphin of France.

At 12 years old, Archduchess Maria Antonia was the ideal age for marriage and had been drilled from an early age in preparation for her future career as a royal consort. Happily, she had survived smallpox unscathed and it was with a certain maternal pride that Maria Theresa presented her daughter to Étienne François, Duke of Choiseul, making the first move in negotiating the marriage that would end beneath the blade.

Equally keen to cement relations between his own nation and Austria, Choiseul returned to France full of enthusiasm for this suggested match, sure it would mend the damage wrought by the Seven Years' War. This was no whirlwind courtship and it was only after two long years of delicate negotiation that the deal was struck. An enormous dowry of two hundred thousand crowns was agreed upon and the family of the groom-to-be turned a critical eye on the now teenage archduchess.

Maria Antonia did not, it was decided, look the part of a dauphine at all; if she were to join the house of Bourbon, then something must be done. Her wardrobe was easy enough to change and soon the carefree girl was dressed to the height of French fashion, slowly morphing from child to bride to be. No doubt she looked forward to this new adventure with a mixture of excitement and apprehension but there was one particularly unpleasant trial yet to face and it was something that nobody could enjoy.

Although Maria Antonia had received an education of sorts and was a particularly gifted harpist, this talent paled when weighed against her appearance, and the French court found her teeth and smile most offensive of all. If changing her style of dress had been an inconvenience, then changing her teeth would be nothing short of agonizing. Still, the empress was set on the path of marriage and dentist Pierre Laveran was summoned and set to work correcting the archduchess's teeth. Months of painful, unanesthetized procedures followed, employing an early form of dental brace. Maria Antonia endured the discomfort with fortitude until the families of bride and groom declared themselves satisfied, no doubt to the tormented girl's immense relief.

Now she certainly had a smile fit for Versailles but her hair, make up and knowledge of the strict etiquette of the Bourbon court were found wanting. Once again the young lady had to endure some arduous self-improvement. Etiquette would become an ongoing battle even after her wedding and the dauphine was famously made to submit to the ministrations of Anne d'Arpajon, Countess Noailles, as her lady-in-waiting. Anne had previously served Marie Leszczyńska and was considered an expert in courtly behaviour; indeed, the Dauphine would come to despise the stuffy Anne and even nicknamed her *Madame Etiquette*, seeing her as a figurehead for the sort of stuffy, unyielding propriety that she abhorred.

For now, though, Maria Antonia was not a queen, not even a dauphine, and had no choice but to go along with all that was asked of her until, finally, it was agreed that she might pass muster.

On 19 April 1770, Maria Antonia and her brother, Ferdinand, attended the Augustinian Church in Vienna. Here she was married to Louis by proxy and the girl who entered the church as Archduchess Maria Antonia left it as Marie Antoinette, Dauphine of France. This lady of Versailles was by now the ripe old age of 14 and life as an adult was about to begin. She left Vienna for France two days later and was introduced for the first time to Madame Etiquette, who was to accompany the young bride to meet her groom.

On 14 May, after a long and arduous journey as part of an enormous procession of coaches, the young newlyweds laid eyes on one another for the first time in a misty forest clearing near Compiegne. Marie Antoinette threw herself at the feet of her husband and his grandfather, Louis XV, and the dauphin gently raised her to stand and escorted her to his own carriage, in which she made the remainder of the journey to her new life.

Marie Antoinette and Louis were finally married in person on 16 May 1770 in a stunning ceremony at the royal chapel of Versailles, the bride dressed in a gown bedecked with pearls and diamonds. Despite the magnificence of the dress and its dramatic train all was not well and Elizabeth Percy, Duchess of Northumberland, commented in her famous diaries that not only were the royal princesses greedy to a turn, but Marie Antoinette's gown was too small, leaving much of her shift visible at the back. Still, despite this sartorial blunder, the wedding passed off in fine style before a crowd of five thousand that was crammed into grandstands in the Hall of Mirrors. Here the cream of society watched the procession pass and witnessed the dawn of one of the most famous marriages in European royal history.

When Marie Antoinette signed her name to the register a blot of ink dripped onto the page, obscuring part of her signature whilst outside the palace, a violent storm raged. All of this was taken as an omen of ill things to come by some who witnessed the wedding but for most, the day was a roaring success. After a day of feasting and celebration the pair were escorted in time-honoured tradition to the marital bed where they fell into an exhausted slumber, with the business of producing an heir left for another time. The following morning Louis was up and about early to go hunting, hardly the most romantic start to a honeymoon.

Although the groom spent his first day as a married man out with his friends in pursuit of game, a terrible catastrophe provided the tragic coda to the celebrations. In the years that followed many came to interpret this disaster as a bad omen for the royal marriage, though it was arguably far worse for those directly in the very literal line of fire...

Two weeks after the marriage, on 30 May, the people of Paris gathered in the Place Louis XV to attend a festival in celebration of the marriage. A wonderful fete was planned at which drink would flow, entertainers would promenade and fireworks would delight the audience.

By all accounts the night was a triumph until, as the evening winds blew stronger, tragedy struck. Caught in a strong gust of wind, newly launched fireworks were swept into stores of unlit rockets and the entire arsenal exploded, shooting into the tightly-packed crowd. Specially-erected wooden stalls caught alight, grandstands collapsed and the audience flew into a quite understandable panic. As they tried to flee the raging flames the hysterical crowd found that they were hemmed in, their only possible escape route being along the Rue Royale.

Blinded by smoke and panic the crowd surged into the street only to find themselves confronted by a large group coming in the opposite direction, unaware of the drama unfolding. In the ensuing stampede people were trampled and crushed as the celebrations gave way to tragedy.

After the dead were counted, official estimates claimed that 133 people had lost their lives but unofficial accounts record it as far higher. Hundreds of survivors were left with catastrophic injuries or permanent disabilities and many years later, the disastrous festival was still claiming its victims.

Was it an omen of things to come? That is a matter of belief, but it was certainly no way to start married life and for Louis and Marie Antoinette, it was just the beginning of their many troubles.

A Marriage in Exile

Marie Joséphine of Savoy and Louis XVIII (Savoy, Bourbon)

14 May 1771, Versailles, France

Before we begin to reflect on the somewhat eventful, very rarely happy union of the woman who was born Maria Giuseppina Luigia di Savoia, Princess of Savoy, and Louis Stanislas, Count of Provence and later Louis XVIII, it seems only right to give fair warning that we will be meeting the bride again later in our chapter on royal scandals. That will give you a clue into just how things went between Louis Stanislas and Maria, who took the name Marie Joséphine at her marriage.

The daughter of Infanta Maria Antonia Ferdinanda of Spain and Prince Victor Amadeus of Savoy, heir to the throne of Sardinia, Marie Joséphine was raised in preparation for a good marriage and on 16 April 1771, she secured it. On this day, she was married by proxy to the Count of Provence, Prince Louis Stanislas of France. As brother of the dauphin, the prince was within a hair's breadth of the throne itself and winning his hand in marriage was no mean feat, bringing the house of Savoy to the forefront of European royal power. Immediately after the wedding Marie Joséphine was whisked away from the Kingdom of Sardinia and arrived in France a month later to make the acquaintance of her new husband, the pinnacle of several marriages that had been contracted between the two kingdoms.

The houses of Savoy and Bourbon were united in person at a grand ceremony that was held at Versailles on 14 May 1771. For days afterwards festivities celebrated the union, culminating in a grand ball in honour of the new couple. Once the party was over and the guests went home, however, it soon became apparent that things were far from rosy at Versailles.

Chief among the concerns Louis Stanislas had about his new wife was her somewhat questionable personal hygiene. Marie Joséphine did not particularly like to bathe, nor did she regularly clean her teeth and, faced with her disinterest in cleanliness, her new husband flatly refused to consummate the marriage. Of course, whether he was capable of doing so was also the subject of some whispering at court, so perhaps this excuse was just what he had been looking for.

Perhaps unsurprisingly given her singular ways, in the etiquette and gossip-driven hothouse of Versailles, Marie Joséphine was far from popular. Measured against the carefully cultivated style, poise and even teeth of her sister-in-law, Marie Antoinette, Marie Joséphine found herself targeted as a figure of fun by those loyal to the Austrian dauphine. Her position was little helped when her husband, well aware that his brother and Marie Antoinette had yet to consummate their own marriage, boasted of his entirely fictitious yet apparently voracious sexual exploits with his new wife, rather a risque move for a royal prince. However, Louis Stanislas went too far when he falsely claimed that Marie Joséphine was already pregnant, which would have been the ultimate coup over his brother. The courtiers of Versailles no doubt laughed behind their hands at such a fanciful tale and when no baby came along, the story soon faded into red-faced fiction.

Eventually, however, Louis Stanislas and Marie Joséphine put their mutual dissatisfaction aside and in 1774 the couple announced that the Countess of Provence really was pregnant. Sadly the good news was short-lived and the pregnancy ended in miscarriage, as did a second in 1781. The couple remained childless for the rest of their marriage.

There was, however, one thing that *could* unite Marie Joséphine and Louis Stanislas and that was a shared dislike of Marie Antoinette and her husband, Louis. The animosity was more than mutual, with both sides plotting and gossiping against each other, egged on by delighted courtiers. Of course, being the heir to a throne does wonders for one's popularity and the dauphin and dauphine certainly enjoyed far more support among their canny followers. Marie Joséphine's unhappy situation and isolated state was further complicated when Louis Stanislas took as mistress his wife's lady-in-waiting, Anne Nompar de Caumont, Countess of Balbi,.

Although royal mistresses were hardly unheard of, Marie Joséphine was disappointed that her loyal retainer had been tempted into her husband's bed. However, recognizing the truism that revenge is best served cold, Marie Joséphine waited out her retaliation for this particular slight. She kept Anne in her service at Versailles even as the couple's marriage became even more strained and, when Louis Stanislas and Marie Joséphine finally went their separate ways years later, Marie Joséphine insisted that Anne remain in her service, thus scuppering her husband's hopes of cosying up to his mistress on the continent.

It took the storm clouds of the French Revolution to end the unhappy domestic situation and when the two royal couples left Versailles for Paris in 1789, Louis and Marie Antoinette established their family and courtiers at the Tuileries whilst Marie Joséphine and Louis Stanislas took up residence in the Luxembourg Palace. When the doomed royal family made their famed and failed flight to Varennes in June 1791, the bickering Provences somehow made a successful escape, finding refuge in the Austrian Netherlands and, later, Germany.

It was at this point that the royal marriage, never loving, devoted or even particularly tolerant, split apart completely. Whilst Louis Stanislas would eventually accompany the French court into exile under the shelter of Tsar Paul I, Marie Joséphine established herself in Schleswig-Holstein. The tale of how a trip to visit her estranged husband proved disastrous is one I shall tell in our romp through royal scandals but for now, the marriage was effectively over. Husband and wife were in different countries and for Louis Stanislas, fate had one last card to play.

Louis Stanislas was never expected to sit on the throne of France yet the violent and unexpected forces of the Revolution changed lives in the most unexpected ways. The king, of course, died on the guillotine and his heir, Louis XVII, died in prison in 1795, no more than a child. Safe in exile Louis Stanislas was proclaimed king by his supporters, though his queen was not by his side and would not be for many years.

Henry and the Widow Horton

Anne Horton and Prince Henry, Duke of Cumberland and Strathearn (Hanover)

2 October 1771, London, England

With actresses, widows and scandalous sorts warming the beds of the heirs to the throne, one could be forgiven for thinking that the gentlemen of the house of Hanover had something of a weakness for unsuitable ladies. Some found their marriage plans confounded by the Royal Marriages Act, but what of the man whose actions caused it to be necessary in the first place?

For that, one can thank Prince Henry, Duke of Cumberland and Strathearn, and brother of George III. His own assignation with a lady of questionable reputation left his crowned sibling so incensed that he finally reached the end of his patience and put his foot down, quite something for George. It was a last ditch attempt to ensure that such a scandal could never happen again, though in the face of true love and fanciful romance, his efforts were destined to fail.

The lady who turned Prince Henry's head was born Anne Luttrell in 1743, daughter of Simon Luttrell, Member of Parliament and later the Earl of Carhampton. The young Anne was considered something of a catch so it came as a surprise to society when she eschewed her finer suitors and married a commoner and squire, Christopher Horton. Horton's death cut short the marriage and, before four years had passed, Anne was a widow. Young and glamorous, she was in no mood to sit and mope so after a suitable period of mourning, Mrs Horton was once again on the market.

One thing the widow Horton was very good at was making friends and, with her commoner husband dead and gone, she returned to the London society that was her natural home. Here she became, as Horace Walpole commented waspishly, 'the Duke of Grafton's Mrs Hoghton, the Duke of Dorset's Mrs Hoghton, everyone's Mrs Hoghton'.[11] However, Anne wasn't about to be content in friendships with the likes of Dorset and Grafton when, through her social circle, she had met a prince.

On 2 October 1771, just three years after she became a widow, Anne Horton, née Luttrell, married Henry, the Duke of Cumberland and Strathearn, at her home in Hertford Street, London. So far, you might think, so normal. After all, it's hardly stolen diamonds, leggy actresses and ten illegitimate children, but the king was incensed. Not only was Anne a commoner by birth, she had already been married once and her reputation was anything but unblemished. She was nowhere near George's idea of the ideal bride for his brother and as far as he was concerned, such a marriage should never be able to take place again. For that reason, the Royal Marriages Act was created.

In fact, the Act proved difficult to enforce and we shall see more of the marriages that it failed to prevent elsewhere in this volume. Act of Parliament and furious brother or not, Henry was in love with Anne and he flatly refused to turn his back on his bride. Buoyed by the support of her husband, Anne pushed for official recognition as a princess, not content with being a mere duchess. It was an audacious and ultimately hopeless case as there was never a realistic chance that she might be awarded such a grand title given her brother-in-law's opposition to the marriage. After all, to give Anne the recognition of a title such as princess would have undermined the Royal Marriages Act as well as the royal authority; it would be tantamount to an acceptance of this most unsuitable marriage and George would never agree to that.

Following a continental tour, Anne and Henry established a salon at Cumberland House that became the talk of the town, with Anne exuding charm and ready wit to all who came into her exalted circle. This unofficial court proved wildly popular until Cumberland's ill health forced them to quit London for Brighton in 1779 although they continued to enjoy the high life, swiftly working their way through their finances thanks to European jaunts and a whirlwind of social engagements.

Their childless marriage came to an end in 1790 with the duke's death, yet still Anne's spending didn't slow and bit by bit she was forced to sell off her late husband's belongings to settle her mounting debts. By now in her late forties, her illustrious followers had long since moved on, leaving Anne with only her bills and memories of a time long passed. Eventually, she left England for the continent where she died at Gorizia on 28 December 1808, her scandalous career at an end.

A Marriage Denied

Maria Fitzherbert and George IV (Hanover)

15 December 1785, London, England

In 1785 two people, deeply in love and united by devotion, were married at the bride's house in Park Street, in the fashionable Mayfair district of London. In a departure from the usual routine for members of the groom's illustrious family, the ceremony was not presided over by the Archbishop of Canterbury but the Reverend Robert Burt, one of the Chaplains in Ordinary to the Prince of Wales. The bride was Maria Fitzherbert, née Smythe, a 29-year-old, twice-widowed Roman Catholic woman and the groom none other than George, Prince of Wales, the man who would one day rule as Prince Regent and, eventually, King George IV.

The marriage was a scandal in the making and a secret to be kept, forbidden in law by the Royal Marriages Act of 1772. The wilful George had no care for the Act that rendered his marriage null and void and had neither sought nor gained permission from his father, George III, for this most forbidden union. Not only that but, even if he *had* approached the king and somehow secured the monarch's agreement for the wedding, then the prince and and any children that resulted from the marriage would have been forever disqualified from wearing the crown. That Act, as we have learned already, ruled that no person who converted to Roman Catholicism or married a Catholic could ever inherit the throne of Britain yet here was the heir to that very throne throwing caution to the wind in pursuit of one of his many romantic conquests. Still, perhaps the young prince was working on the assumption that it is easier to seek forgiveness than ask permission and so, as he did so often in his eventful life, the Prince of Wales simply carried on regardless.

How, though, did the heir to the British throne come to meet this lady from Shropshire, and what was the road that led to this infamous union?

The woman who went down in history as Mrs Fitzherbert was born Maria Anne Smythe and married her first husband, Edward Weld, when she was just 19. Three months later, an equestrian accident left the new bride a widow, but not one of means. In his thirties, Weld had not considered that death might be looming and had not got around to putting his paperwork in any sort of order. Instead of leaving his new wife well cared for all she inherited was an unsigned will, whilst his considerable estate passed to his brother, leaving Maria with nothing but memories of a very short marriage indeed.

Still, Maria was not a lady to let life get her down and within three years had secured herself a second husband, Thomas Fitzherbert. Once again the fates were not smiling on Maria's love life and three years after the marriage, she was a widow once more but this time the newly bereaved lady found herself with a generous payout and a house in Mayfair. Now financially secure and still only 24-years-old, Maria spread her social wings and was soon a leading light in the most illustrious circles in the capital, often as the guest of her half-uncle, Charles William Molyneux, Earl of Sefton.

It was whilst attending the opera with Lord Sefton in 1784 that Maria was first introduced to the Prince of Wales, surely the pinnacle of her social ambition. For George it was love or at least infatuation at first sight and he decided that this was the lady for him. Mrs Fitzherbert, somewhat worldlier, and definitely less romantic, did not share the 22-year-old prince's infatuation and was sure that his interest would soon wane. After all, George's reputation preceded him and being pursued by the flighty prince was hardly a novelty for ladies of London society. When George sent Mrs Fitzherbert jewellery, she promptly returned it; in reply, the devastated young man sent word that he had attempted suicide and languished on the threshold of death. She must come to Carlton House with all haste, he begged, and see him one last time.

It is perhaps surprising that the worldly Maria fell for this ploy but fall for it she did and the shocked lady hurried to the royal bedside. Here she found George pale, weak and, one must say, theatrical. He implored her to take a borrowed ring and when she did so, told the lady and those present that her acceptance of the gift constituted their betrothal. As soon as she reached home, Maria returned the ring and made preparations to leave England and the insistent prince far behind her.

Most people might take the hint if the object of their affections fled the country and headed for Europe, but young George was not most people and when Maria made her getaway his affection only deepened. Retainers gave chase, letters were exchanged and through a combination of tenacity and old-fashioned romance, George finally managed to woo his Maria.

Upon her return to England, Maria and George entered into a morganatic, secret and illegal marriage. The couple were wed at Maria's home on 15 December 1785 before her uncle and brother in a ceremony officiated by the aforementioned Reverend Burt. Though rumours persist that Burt was an inmate of the Fleet Prison who was released only after George had settled his debts, the reverend came from a wealthy family and the records of the Fleet Prison contain no mention of his name. After all, it's unlikely that a man with such a history would have reached the dizzying ecclesiastical heights of Chaplain in Ordinary to the Prince of Wales.

Maria and George settled into a surprisingly loving marriage, given his propensity for a roaming eye and romance. In the years that they were together as man and wife, London gossips assumed that Maria was nothing more than another royal mistress, a belief that George was happy to encourage. After all, it was in his best interests to string his father and Parliament along and they continued to settle his ever-increasing debts on the understanding that one day he would marry and secure the line of succession for the house of Hanover.

Those debts, however, showed no signs of shrinking as George continued with his devil-may-care approach to life and in 1787, utterly drowning in debt, the prince left Carlton House and moved into Maria's home on Park Street whilst trying to negotiate a further financial grant from Parliament. Despite the King's distaste at his son's close ties to Charles James Fox, the Whig leader brokered a deal with George, securing him the cash he needed in return for a public denial of the widespread rumours that he was married to a Catholic widow. In dire straits, George put money ahead of the woman he had once adored and agreed to the deal.

On 30 April 1787, Fox stood before the House of Commons and gave a speech on the matter of the prince's debts that included the following passage, its meaning in little doubt:

'[The rumours of marriage] …proved at once the uncommon pains taken by the enemies of his Royal Highness to propagate the grossest and most malignant falsehoods with a view to depreciate his character and injure him in the opinion of his country. [...] a tale in every particular so unfounded, and for which there was not the shadow of anything like reality.'[12]

Furthermore, the prince was happy to offer his 'fullest assurances of the utter falsehood of the fact in question, which never had, and which common sense must see, never could have happened.'[13]

Fox's words were carefully chosen but for those who heard the speech there was no doubt as to what the 'fact in question' might be nor of the identity of the lady concerned. For all Fox's delicacy of language, the damage was done and Maria was furious at what she understandably saw as a betrayal. She was probably very likely glad to put some space between herself and her lover, who moved back into Carlton House nearly £170,000 better off. Perhaps George really did see no damage in telling such a falsehood in order to save his financial skin but equally, might we be generous and wonder if he did not consider it a lie at all? After all, the marriage was *not* legal, as it had not received the blessing of the king and it might be that George was viewing its legalities in these strict terms. Of course, he could simply have been saying the best thing to guarantee a generous payout but whatever his motive, his wife was resolutely unimpressed.

All of this was a public relations disaster and George sank in the public's affection to a new low from which he would struggle to recover. On top of that, a constitutional crisis was just waiting to happen. In 1788, George III was experiencing his first prolonged bout of mental illness and despite endless and ever more debilitating treatments, his condition showed no sign of improving. With the disturbed king foaming at the mouth and incoherent, he was in no fit state to deliver his speech for the State Opening of Parliament. This meant that, although Members of Parliament could meet and discuss business, anything that arose from such discussions could not be considered an official parliamentary decision until the king's speech had been given.

As time marched on the situation grew more dire and MPs met to discuss the possibility of establishing a Regency. Although a Regency Bill was drawn up by Pitt, negotiations on all sides delayed its passing long enough for the king to recover his wits. As the prince's first opportunity for power slipped away he seemed little concerned, far more preoccupied with the fact that Maria had forgiven him all over again. Content to be settled once more on her loving bosom and with his debts in the hands of Parliament, all was rosy for the charmed and charming prince, who had by now taken something of a liking to the south coast. Setting up individual residences in Brighton, George and Maria sat at the heart of fashionable society, hosting some of the most illustrious names in the country whilst at his father's *official* court, things were less than happy.

George and Charlotte loathed the open liaisons between their son and his Catholic lover and one is tempted to speculate that they might well have suspected the marriage despite Fox's very public denials. Both the king and queen were intelligent people and they knew their son and his ways very well, leaving them in no doubt that a morganatic marriage was just the sort of thing that might appeal to him. Of course, the marriage had no legal status without the permission of the king and Privy Council but this would have been scant comfort to his parents. Once again though the happy ever after was not to last and George's fancies were taken by others, as Maria struggled to retain her allure now that she was a more permanent fixture in his life.

Almost ten years after the wedding, George sent a letter to Maria in which he explained that their marriage must end. With no excuses left and Parliament and king tired of delays, the time had finally come for him to make an official and, as we will soon discover, disastrous marriage. To further complicate matters, George had started a romantic liaison with Frances Villiers, Countess of Jersey, and she strongly counselled him to do as his parents wished and marry Caroline of Brunswick, an arrangement that would get rid of his mountain of debt and clear the temptation of Maria away forever. Lady Jersey was understandably keen on retaining her status as senior royal mistress and quite rightly deduced that Caroline posed less of a threat to her position than Maria. However, despite the official marriage, it was to Maria that George willed all his possessions, not his loathed wife nor the cunning Lady Jersey.

Maria was heartbroken by the end of the marriage and George was devastated too, despite the cynicism behind his decision. Though the couple attempted to reconcile once his disastrous marriage to Caroline of Brunswick collapsed, the happy times they had known were far behind them as too much heartache had come between the couple to be easily forgotten. George's open affection for Isabella Ingram-Seymour-Conway, Marchioness of Hertford, was the final straw that destroyed their reconciliation.

In public George ignored Maria, openly favouring Lady Hertford and when he snubbed her at a dinner at Carlton House in 1811, telling her to sit away from him 'according to her rank', the relationship collapsed. Maria and George never met again and as the years wore on what had once been love turned to animosity. Maria threatened to expose their marriage if she did not receive an annuity whilst George came to believe she had married him only for advancement but in truth, this cannot have been the case. She already enjoyed social standing and financial stability and being the illegal, unrecognized spouse of George brought little to Maria that she could not have achieved elsewhere by making a good, *legal* marriage. Admittedly she was treated like a queen during their years in Brighton, but it was an uncertain position and for a woman seeking advancement, a legal marriage to one a little less notorious would have been a far safer bet.

When Maria heard that George was unwell in 1830 she sent him a final note; too weakened by illness to respond, he cherished it to the end. Unaware of the perilous state of her former lover's health, Maria was bitterly hurt that he did not reply, learning too late that he had simply been too unwell to pen a response. Before George's death, he asked to be buried with Maria's eye miniature, a token of their earlier devotion, around his neck. This final wish was granted, perhaps proving how deeply George rued the loss of his first wife, Mrs Fitzherbert.

A Match Made in Hell

Caroline of Brunswick and George IV (Brunswick-Bevern, Hanover)
8 April 1795, London, England

Like all couples who venture into the unchartered waters of holy matrimony, our royal players could have no guarantee of a happy ending. Should things go wrong the best they could hope for was a public scandal to relieve them of their marital ties, whilst the worst might be decades of misery, yoked to a spouse one was bound to come to resent. And if they were really unlucky, they might even end their days incarcerated. In these modern times, nobody is particularly shocked when a royal marriage ends in divorce but one might hope that the participants at least had a modicum of affection for one another at the start of their journey.

Certainly, when the latest royal couple leaves the altar at St Paul's or Westminster Abbey they are not, one imagines, anywhere close to echoing George's first impression of Caroline. He is reported to have said that he found it almost impossible to 'overcome the disgust of her person'.[14] Indeed, on their very first meeting, he declared himself so unwell that he needed wine and plenty of it so hopes were not high when, on 8 April 1795, George and Caroline met in the Chapel Royal of St James's Palace. These cousins were not there because of love or respect and they were hardly what could be termed friends. Though both had their reasons for agreeing to the unfortunate match, the groom harboured no illusions that he would be happy as a result of it. Still, one cannot help but think that Caroline, who appeared to Lady Maria Stuart to be 'in the highest spirits',[15] might have at least been willing to give it a go.

The groom agreed to the marriage because he had literally no other choice if he wished to avoid financial ruin. Wracked by debt and a profligate spender, George's father, George III, had finally reached the end of his tether and left his son with an ultimatum: no marriage, no money. Of course, the prince's heart rested firmly in the shapely bosom of his illegal bride, Maria Fitzherbert, and his loins had rested in a good many other places besides, but none of these comforts were about to pay out to the tune required to clear his debts.

If George at least got to have fun at the gaming table building up the debts that now weighed so heavily on his shoulders, for Caroline things were a lot more proper. The house of Brunswick-Bevern looked on the marriage as a piece of social and political climbing par excellence and was thrilled to see its daughter joining such an illustrious family. Not far off 30, Caroline was no blushing teen bride and more than one contemporary commented on her somewhat casual attitude towards personal hygiene. Still, she very likely hoped that her marriage would at least be a friendly one and might one day perhaps blossom into something more romantic.

Needless to say, the bride was to face an immense disappointment and it began almost immediately. Whilst George declared himself overcome by Caroline and complained that she made him feel unwell, the lady lamented that her husband to be was not at all like his portrait. One can only imagine the alarm bells that must have been ringing at this point but the deal had been struck and the road to marriage was set. Just to be sure that Caroline could not misunderstand his intentions, George established Frances, Countess of Jersey, as his fiancé's Lady of the Bedchamber. Lady Jersey was unashamedly the prince's senior mistress and she was of no mind to make Caroline's life in England easy. Under the hawkish eye of the countess, Caroline spent three days preparing for the wedding day, keenly aware of Lady Jersey's place in her fiancé's life.

Still, on the big day itself, the bride was determined to at least look the part and she appeared at the palace resplendent in silver and ermine, bedecked in a robe of crimson velvet, no doubt to Lady Jersey's delight. George, however, was far less of a mind to make a go of things and he staggered into the ceremony drunk to the point of insensibility. Tottering here and there as the Archbishop of Canterbury, the Most Reverend John Moore attempted to keep things on track, George eventually had to be held up by his groomsmen, the Dukes of Bedford and Roxburghe, simply to keep him on his feet. However, neither Roxburghe nor Bedford were able to provide such a stabilizing influence in the bedroom and when the couple retired to their chamber, George collapsed in a drunken stupor. As Caroline commented later: 'What it was to have a drunken husband on one's wedding-day, and one who passed the greater part of his bridal night under the grate where he fell, and where I left him.'[16]

It was an inauspicious start to a disastrous marriage. Just months after the birth of their only child, Princess Charlotte, the following year, George cut his wife out of his life. From that day the couple would never reconcile but Caroline wasn't about to go quietly. Instead she decided to conduct a little scandal of her own, as we will discover in the next chapter.

The Princess Who Got Away

Charlotte, Princess Royal and The Hereditary Prince Frederick I of Württemberg (Hanover, Württemberg)

18 May 1797, London, England

Charlotte, Princess Royal, was, her sisters thought, the lucky one.

Whilst the daughters of George III and Queen Charlotte were left at home to care for their tired mother, as she in turn cared for their ailing father, Charlotte left England and her parents far behind. The princess was fortunate indeed to make her match before her father's mental illness took its toll, for once it did, the decision was made to gather the royal daughters to their mother's bosom and there would be no more brides from the British court for many a long year. Of course, by the time that sad state of affairs came about, Charlotte was already embarking on a brand new life.

Charlotte was the fourth child and first daughter of the king and queen and her status as Princess Royal meant that she was destined from birth to be one of the key players in a suitably grand dynastic marriage. Her parents were ecstatic to have a girl join their growing family and before she was 2 years old, Charlotte's education began, training her in earnest for the fate that awaited her. As a child she developed a dislike for the more public side of being a royal princess, all of which she bore with the occasional grumble and a certain cool detachment.

Keen to be married, Charlotte found the field of possible husbands massively reduced by her father's decision that his children would not marry into a Catholic family under any circumstances. However, the suitor most favoured by the princess was not only the son of a Catholic, he was also a man with scandal in his past.

The Hereditary Prince Frederick of Württemberg was a widower and father of three who had been accused of infidelity and abuse by his late wife, Duchess Augusta of Brunswick-Wolfenbüttel. So severe was his treatment of her, she claimed, she had been left with no choice but to flee her husband and take refuge in Russia.

Mindful of these lurid allegations as well as his Catholic connections, the king and queen initially refused permission for the marriage. Charlotte, however, pursued the matter with her characteristic determination and eventually won the all-important blessing of her father, which her mother was duty bound to accept.

The wedding took place on 18 May 1797 at the Chapel Royal of St James's Palace with celebrations going on for days before the newlyweds set off for their new home in Stuttgart. Despite Frederick's fearsome reputation, Charlotte saw no sign of the monstrous figure who had terrorized Augusta, and the couple enjoyed a peaceful marriage. Although their only child was stillborn, Charlotte's stepchildren adored her and she was devoted to them in turn, treating them as her own. Free from the confines of Windsor and the realities of being just one princess among many, Charlotte blossomed in Stuttgart and made new friends wherever she went.

Life in the eighteenth century courts was nothing if not eventful and the peaceful Stuttgart court was to suffer a serious shake-up in 1800 when French troops marched into Württemberg. As soldiers entered the city, the duke and duchess fled for the safety of Vienna where, to the horror of Charlotte's parents, Frederick allied with Napoleon. In return for his allegiance and his agreement to numerous territorial exchanges, Frederick was initially given the title of Elector of Württemberg in 1803. His devotion was further rewarded in 1805 when the elector and electress became King and Queen of Württemberg, ruling from their home at the Ludwigsburg Palace.

Although Frederick switched sides once again in 1813, Charlotte's parents found it hard to reconcile the political behaviour of their daughter and the son-in-law they had never really wanted in the first place. Indeed, George flatly refused to address Charlotte as Queen of Württemberg, even after the title was confirmed by the Congress of Vienna. In keeping with Charlotte's pragmatic approach to life, she took this new development in her stride and when Frederick died in 1816, the Dowager Queen remained at the palace they had shared, receiving noble visitors from across Europe.

Amongst those who flocked to visit Ludwigsburg were some of Charlotte's own siblings, a clear confirmation that George's disgust at her behaviour had not extended throughout the entire family. Although she made her home in Germany, the Queen of Württemberg did return to England just once after her marriage when, in 1827, she visited the land of her birth to undergo surgery for dropsy. Perhaps after so long away it felt as foreign as Germany once had because she returned home to the continent the following year. Here she remained until her death, a long way from the little girl who had been born in Buckingham House.

'The next best thing'

Princess Charlotte of Wales and Leopold I of Belgium (Hanover, Saxe-Coburg and Gotha)

2 May 1816, London, England

Once upon a time there lived an unhappy princess; an only child, she was witty, bright and longed for a little excitement, perhaps even a little love. She was not quite kept prisoner in a tower on the edge of the forest but she was isolated from society and family alike at Cranbourne Lodge, where her resentment of her notorious father festered and grew. This fairytale, sadly, does not have a happy ending, but the unhappy princess and her Prince Charming gave it a very good shot.

Princess Charlotte of Wales was the only child born to the Prince of Wales, later to be George IV, and his loathed and estranged wife, Caroline of Brunswick. At the age of 18, this most eligible young lady remained unmarried, dissatisfied and at odds with her father, who had set his sights on a match between his daughter and William, Prince of Orange. She was determined that she would never capitulate to the marriage yet she had reckoned without George, who always got his own way. Her father was as tenacious as he was profligate and kept up his entreaties until, in 1814 Charlotte reluctantly signed the marriage contract that promised her to William.

Charlotte's mother, however, made no secret of her opposition to the betrothal. Caroline enjoyed immense public support after her own marriage to George collapsed and the people of England rallied to Caroline's call.

Soon Charlotte found herself supported by a public chorus that echoed her own dissatisfaction, all of whom wanted their princess to remain in England.

Betrothed she might be, but like her father, Charlotte's eye kept on wandering. Although George took so many mistresses they could fill a book of their own, Charlotte's cosseted status meant that she could only admire from afar, which she did with aplomb. The princess developed an attachment to a mysterious, anonymous Prussian gentleman yet, ever the realist, she declared that she would be happy to take 'the next best thing, which was a good tempered man with good sense',[17] should the Prussian in question not return her affections. Whoever the mystery figure was, he apparently did not share her adoration and when Charlotte set eyes on Prince Leopold of Saxe-Coburg-Saalfeld in London, she decided that the future king of Belgium was certainly 'the next best thing', Orange be damned. Unfortunately, George and William of Orange did not agree, but Charlotte had her father's blood running in her veins and she, like her father, did not take no for an answer.

Determined that she would not marry the Prince of Orange, Charlotte made repeated arguments in favour of Leopold to her father. He declared such discussions pointless since she was already promised to William, refusing to even entertain the unthinkable prospect of calling off that illustrious marriage. Charlotte had one last trump card to play and demanded of her husband to be that her mother be allowed to visit the marital home, sure that he would abide by her father's express wishes and refuse the condition. The gamble paid off and when William followed George's example and refused to give permission for Caroline to visit following the marriage, he played right into Charlotte's hands. She could not, Charlotte declared, be happy with a man who would not allow her to see her beloved mother and if he cared so little for her happiness, then how could they possibly be husband and wife? All appeals to her to reconsider were to no avail and Charlotte decided that the engagement must be broken and she must be allowed to marry a man with whom she had at least a chance of happiness.

Faced with such entreaties, George caved in and ended the engagement. Free once more, Charlotte upped her representations on behalf of Leopold, who was fighting on the continent. Although the Prince Regent was far from convinced, when Leopold signalled that he would be happy to consider the matter, George finally relented and invited the young man to Brighton to discuss this most important issue.

The meeting proved to be a wildly successful encounter and George finally gave his blessing to the longed-for union, much to his daughter's relief. The official announcement of the engagement was made in the House of Commons in March 1816 and the people of England met the news with great cheer, deeming Leopold a far more appealing match than William. Never one to miss the opportunity to splash out, the Prince Regent purchased Claremont House and Parliament agreed a salary of £50,000 for Leopold, neatly solving his money worries in one generous swoop.

The party atmosphere continued through spring and on the appointed wedding day of 2 May 1816, the streets of London were thronged with thousands of people who had turned out to mark the happy occasion. Although the wedding ceremony was not scheduled to take place until that evening the day was spent in celebration, a world away from the unhappy experience endured by Charlotte's own parents and when the party filed into the Crimson Drawing Room at Carlton House, there could be no doubt that Charlotte and Leopold had longed for this moment. Charlotte's gown, bought at a cost of more than £10,000, was utterly magnificent and her groom cut a dashing figure in the perfectly turned out uniform of a British General, mindful of the importance of making just the right impression.

As the couple set off for their honeymoon they no doubt looked forward to many happy years together yet fate had other, tragic plans and just a year later, Charlotte would die as she delivered a stillborn child. For now let us leave them happy ever after, starting out on the adventure of the married life they had petitioned so hard to achieve.

The Second Empress

Marie Louise and Napoleon Bonaparte (Habsburg, Bonaparte)
1 April 1810, Paris, France

And so, for our final stop on the road of royal marriage, we meet a man who arguably dominated European history in the first quarter of the nineteenth century. However, for our dip into the Bonaparte private life,

I have chosen not to visit the emperor's tempestuous relationship with Joséphine de Beauharnais but the events that led to his marriage to Marie Louise, Duchess of Parma. She was the lady who played such an important yet absent role in the unhappy childhood of the short-lived Napoleon II, the wife left behind when her husband went into exile. Marie Louise is often something of a footnote in the life of Napoleon who remains, in the greater consciousness, eternally bound to Joséphine yet for a couple whose passion inarguably burned fiercely, how was it that Napoleon and Joséphine ended up parting so unhappily?

After more than a decade of marriage to the woman whose name has become forever linked to his, there was one problem that even a grand passion couldn't overcome: the matter of succession. Although the marriage of Napoleon and Joséphine had survived separation and infidelity on both sides, the cold truth of the matter was that the emperor needed an heir and it seemed that his beloved Joséphine was unable to oblige.

The woman who was once 'more than my soul, […] the one thought of my life'[18] had lost just a little of her lustre and, as months and years passed with no pregnancy to ensure the succession of the house of Bonaparte, Napoleon took decisive action. He was certain that the problem, if there was one, was not of his own making and the pregnancy of his mistress, Eleonore Denuelle, was the final proof that Napoleon needed of his own fertility. He loved Joséphine, of course, yet no amount of affection was as strong as his wish to see the continuation of his name, the preservation of all that he had achieved and divorce seemed the only way forward.

Though she no doubt saw which way the wind was blowing, the divorce devastated Joséphine. Although neither husband nor wife made any secret of their continued affection for one another, the marriage was annulled in January 1810. Despite his sadness at the end of his grand romance, Napoleon was not one to let the grass grow and by the time the annulment was official, he had already begun looking around for possible replacements to fill the empty spot in his bed.

From the available candidates, Napoleon took a particular liking to the dynastic possibilities offered by a marriage to Grand Duchess Anna, sister of Tsar Alexander I. At just 15, Anna was more than a quarter of a century his junior and blanched at the prospect of becoming the new Empress of the

French. Napoleon's earlier designs on her sister, Ekaterina, were frustrated when she swiftly contracted another marriage but for the teenage Anna, there was no alternative suitor waiting in the wings.

Luckily for Anna, both her mother and the powers that be took exception to the scheme and Napoleon, who so rarely found himself told no, pressed on with his schemes regardless. Whilst Sophie Dorothea of Württemberg prevaricated on behalf of her unwilling daughter, Austria made it clear that it was not pleased at the prospect of a union between France and Russia, the two powerful countries between which it was sandwiched. Should they be united by marriage, the future looked decidedly shaky for the country that lay between them and their objections were made loudly and forcefully. The Tsar was equally lukewarm towards the idea and as discussions dragged on, Napoleon's interest began to wander away from Russia.

If Austria had no wish to be stuck between the intermarried nations of Russia and France then its ruler, Emperor Francis II, was far more open to the possibility of forging a union of his own with Napoleon, fancying a little of that power for himself. He was more than happy to entertain Napoleon's overtures towards his 18-year-old daughter, Marie Louise, who remained blissfully unaware that her future was the subject of such delicate negotiations.

Discussions rumbled on and as the divorce in France was finalized, the deal was finally struck: Napoleon would have his Austrian bride. When the bride to be was informed of the forthcoming nuptials in February 1810, she said simply, 'I wish only what my duty commands me to wish'.[19] The words are surprisingly sanguine and can be interpreted in any number of ways but perhaps she was simply realistic about the life of a noble daughter. Her duty was marriage, her father had contracted it and she had no choice but to obey.

Napoleon was as delighted as Marie Louise was stoic and the marriage took place by proxy on 11 March 1810 at the Augustinian Church, Vienna. With no groom by her side, Marie Louise nonetheless enjoyed a lavish celebration in her honour as the teenager suddenly found herself Empress of the French and Queen of Italy.

The bride left Austria on 13 March to travel to France and a fortnight later, at Compiègne, Marie Louise finally laid eyes on her husband for the first time. It must have been a whirlwind for the young lady, newly removed from a sheltered upbringing and thrust into the spotlight. A civil wedding was held on 1 April 1810 and a grand, religious ceremony took place the following day amid great celebration, the emperor sure that he would find his dreams of an heir finally fulfilled.

Despite the cynicism behind the nuptials, the popular Marie Louise won over courtiers and public alike. Though her union with Napoleon never approached the intense passion of his relationship with Joséphine, the couple were fond of one another and, as had been Francis II's intention, the marriage ensured peace between France and Austria. Finally, in 1811, Napoleon was able to greet his heir when the boy who shared his name made his debut to enormous rejoicing, none greater than the emperor's own.

The Last Georgian Monarchs

Adelaide of Saxe-Meiningen and William IV (Saxe-Meiningen, Hanover)

11 July 1818, Kew, England

As we have unhappily discovered, the marriage of George IV and his official wife was an unmitigated disaster for all concerned, whilst his illegitimate marriage to Maria Fitzherbert hardly ended more happily when it went out with a whimper rather than a bang. What then of William and Adelaide, the last king and queen of the Georgian era?

As the years wore on and George III's mental illness grew more pronounced, his periods of lucidity became few and far between until he was in no fit state to make a decision regarding succession. Still, with the Prince Regent getting older and less healthy and with no legitimate heirs waiting in the wings, one of the sons of the ailing king was going to have to fulfil his dynastic duty. Although George could rule as an heirless regent following the death of his only child, the lack of official grandchildren to continue the line was beginning to become cause for concern.

The ailing king had plenty of unofficial grandchildren and William was responsible for a good many of them thanks to his twenty year relationship with actress Dorothea Jordan, but none of these could ever wear the crown. Correctly surmising that his own noble bottom might one day rest on the throne, William had long since bid adieu to Mrs Jordan and now dispatched his brother, Adolphus, Duke of Cambridge, to find him a suitable future queen. Adolphus duly identified their second cousin, Augusta of Hesse-Cassel, as the perfect candidate but her father declined the offer. In reply, Adolphus simply shrugged his shoulders and married her himself, so taken was he by the charming princess.

Europe was not short of possible brides and spurred on by the promise of a fat payment from Parliament if he could come up with respectable candidate, William found his interest piqued by Adelaide of Saxe-Meiningen. She was the 25-year-old daughter of George I, Duke of Saxe-Meiningen and Princess Luise Eleonore of Hohenlohe-Langenburg, and was an intelligent, charming and deeply religious young lady. With no interest in glamour and society, Adelaide preferred to keep herself to herself, so the realization that she might one day be queen alongside a king almost three decades her senior must have come as quite a shock.

Adelaide travelled to London in the summer of 1818, intending to meet her husband to be at Grillon's Hotel on Albemarle Street. No doubt her fingers were firmly crossed; after all, deciding she might have reservations about the wedding *after* her arrival at the hotel would make life considerably more difficult. Still, if the bride to be was resigned to her fate then her future husband certainly sympathized with her plight. He wryly commented that 'she [Adelaide] is doomed, poor, dear innocent young creature, to be my wife'.[20] He resolved there and then that he would do his best to treat her well and that she would not find herself ill-used. Still, such resolutions are easy to make and as our Georgian royals found out, much more difficult to keep.

Upon their arrival at Grillon's, Adelaide and her mother were received by the Prince Regent. That evening William arrived to join them, meeting for the first time the woman who was destined to be his bride.

The ingredients were all in place to create a recipe for disaster: an arranged betrothal, a huge age difference and a marriage to secure a throne and financial settlement, but against all the odds William and Adelaide found one another diverting company. From the start, the new couple got along splendidly and when they married at Kew a few days later, hopes were high for the future. The couple discovered a shared loathing of pomp and ceremony and the ever-patient Adelaide accepted William's legion of illegitimate children without complaint, whilst proving to be a most stabilizing influence for her new husband.

As the Prince Regent drowned in debt the contented couple looked on, no doubt glad for their own more sober circumstances. They soon settled into a happy routine and for a time left England to establish a home in Hanover, where William's character seemed calmer and his temper less easily lost.

When Adelaide fell pregnant the couple were overjoyed, yet happiness was to turn to tragedy and the baby, Charlotte, lived for only a few hours. A miscarriage followed in 1819 but in 1820 an apparently successful pregnancy resulted in the birth of a daughter, Elizabeth, who died just three months later, weakened by bowel disease. A final attempt to start a family resulted in stillborn twins in 1822 and though rumours persisted of pregnancy, there were to be no further official announcements.

By the time of William's accession to the throne in 1830 the couple were once again in England, happily tucked away at Bushy House. Though William was tempted to do away with the coronation ceremony altogether, Adelaide correctly reasoned that the public enjoyed the tradition and William, as he so often did, listened to her counsel.

The coronation of William IV took place before a celebratory crowd, proving that Adelaide was quite right to encourage the traditional pomp that her husband so disliked. At the ceremony on 8 September 1831 the couple won the respect and admiration of all present, especially after the eagerly-reported excesses of William's late brother. If the reign of George IV was marked by profligacy and scandal, William's could hardly have been more different and the couple's popularity initially soared as a result of the late king's largesse.

The unexpectedly happy marriage was to end in 1837 when the king fell gravely ill at Windsor Castle. With his devoted wife at his side, he lingered for almost two weeks until his death on 20 June, leaving Adelaide devastated. Her popularity never dimmed from that day forward and the marriage of William and Adelaide remains one of the most successful of the Georgian era, a most pleasing note for this nuptial history of the Georgian royals to end on.

1. Queen Anne. 1730, John Closterman, after John Faber.

2. Sophia Electress of Hanover, mother of King George I. 1690, RB Peake.

3. King George I. 1722, John Faber, after D Stevens.

4. George Augustus Prince of Wales, later George II. 1724, Godfrey Kneller.

6. Queen Caroline [of Ansbach] and George Prince of Wales. 1765, Robert Pile, after Richard Houston.

5. King George II and Queen Caroline with their ten children. Anonymous.

7. Frederick, Prince of Wales. 1740, C Boit, after Jacobus Houbraken.

8. King George III. 1804, William Beechey.

9. Queen Charlotte. 1777, Benjamin West.

10. Princess Amelia. Arthur Mee, after JS Agar.

11. George III and his family. 1771, Richard
Earlom, after Johann Zoffany.

12. King George III of the
United Kingdom. W Lowry.

13. Charlotte, Her Royal Highness the Princess Royal. 1801, Peltro W Tomkins.

14. King George IV. 1827, Robert Bowyer, after John Bromley.

15. Mrs Fitzherbert. 1792, after Richard Cosway.

16. Her Most Gracious Majesty Caroline [of Brunswick], Queen of England. 1810, T Wageman, after Thomas A Woolnoth.

17. The maid bringing in the breakfast finds the Prince of Wales and Mrs Fitzherbert in a dishevelled state on the morning after their marriage. 1788, James Gillray.

18. A man disappearing into a cracked chamber pot which has the legs of woman; implying the illicit relationship between the Duke of Clarence and Mrs. Jordan. 1791, James Gillray.

19. Caricature of the Introduction of the Duke of Württemberg (afterwards King Frederick I) to George III and Queen Charlotte previous to his Marriage with Charlotte, Princess Royal of England. Anthony Pasquin.

20. Study for the Portrait of Princess Louisa and Queen Caroline Matilda of Denmark. 1767, Francis Cotes.

21. Coronation of King William IV and Queen Adelaide. 1831, William Woolnoth, after George Cattermole.

22. Princess Caroline Matilda, Queen of Denmark. 1771, James Watson, after Francis Cotes.

23. Catherine the Great. J Miller.

24. Johann Friedrich Struensee. Anonymous.

25. Napoléon I and Marie Louise with their newborn son, Napoléon II. Adolphe Roehn.

26. Paul I, Czar of Russia. JE Mansfield.

27. Louis XV. 1741, Antoine Benoist, after Jakob Christoffel Le Blon, after Nicholas Blakey.

28. Louis XIV. 1676, Robert Nanteuil.

29. Marie Leszczynska of Poland, Queen of France. 1728, Laurent Cars, after Carle Van Loo.

30. Louis XVI's farewell from his wife Marie Antoinette and their distressed children. Jean Baptiste Charles Carbonneau, after JR Charlerie.

31. Louis XVI, Marie-Antoinette, and Louis-Charles. 1793, Jacob Adam, after Antoine-François Callet.

32. Frederick the Great, King of Prussia. 1788, Henri Marais, after Anton Graff.

Act Three

Scandal

'...to propagate scandal, requires neither labour nor courage.'

Samuel Johnson, 1751

As these pages have already shown, the journey from a celebrated birth to a royal wedding could be perilously brief and the path from respectability to scandal for our eighteenth century monarchs had the capacity to be even shorter. In a world where weddings were contracted to save territory, unite fractured diplomatic relations or simply to secure an heir, it is hardly surprising that the royal courts were no stranger to romantic and sexual intrigue. Of course, in the cosseted hothouses of palace life, scandal could not be kept secret for long and once the truth was out, it raged like wildfire through courts that were fuelled by gossip.

Life would be very dull indeed if everyone played by the rules, and for our Georgian monarchs, there were times when excessive philandering or a badly matched couple led to scandalous tales that are still being told today. The man who would become George IV played host to a veritable harem of mistresses and marital discord that culminated in a dramatic public embarrassment at Westminster Abbey, whilst in Denmark, a passionate and powerful affair ended in execution and imprisonment.

Not all of these scandals were extra-marital and some were the result of true love that simply could not be acknowledged, with future kings setting up home with actresses who they could never marry, a sure recipe for sadness. There was also the packed diary of an empress who took lover after lover without shame, though her bedroom remained utterly free of horses whatever the scandalmongers might claim.

For those who prefer their scandals a little more criminal in nature, a doomed queen of France found herself at the centre of a disastrous enterprise thanks to a priceless necklace and the cunning of an ambitious lady of the court. That's without mentioning the sad tale of a secret love between a lonely princess and her father's retainer, or the feuding father and son who simply could not see eye to eye even when death threatened to split them forever.

So prepare to be scandalized... for the Georgian royals did nothing by halves.

A Diplomatic Distraction

Stop for a moment and try to imagine any twenty-first century ruler getting away with half the things our eighteenth century nobles seemed to get up to without making the entire world sit up and blink in amazement. Of course, modern leaders probably do have their indiscretions, but one imagines that they are just far more discreet about it in these media savvy times. Subtle, however, was not in the vocabulary of our next leading lady and though her tale is one of affairs, favourites and supposedly illegitimate sons, her sheer power and influence kept the lid firmly on any scandals that might emerge. For while a king to take official mistresses might have been perfectly normal, for Catherine the Great, however, one man was *never* going to be enough.

Catherine was not always Great, of course; in fact, she wasn't even always Catherine. Born Sophia Augusta Frederica of Anhalt-Zerbst, she was 16-years-old when she changed her name to Catherine and married her second cousin, the future Peter III, Emperor and Autocrat of all the Russias.

Far from a happy marriage, mutual indifference turned to loathing, with neither finding contentment nor companionship in the company of the other. Unfulfilled with a husband who still played with toy soldiers, enthusiastically recreating battles on the marital bed, Catherine looked elsewhere for stimulation both intellectual and sexual. She had no time for childish games and wanted something a little more lusty.

For nine long years the marriage was childless and then, to the relief of the court, it seemed that Peter had put away his toys as Catherine gave birth to a son, who would grow to become the ill-fated Emperor Paul I. There was, of course, the small matter of paternity given Catherine's affairs, but so long as the child was a boy, his future was safe: illegitimate or not, a son secured the all-important line of succession. Never one for diplomacy, when Catherine wrote her memoirs she claimed that she and Peter never consummated their marriage at all so there was no possibility that her husband had fathered her son.

According to the indiscreet empress, she instead found comfort in the arms of her chamberlain, Count Sergei Vasilievich Saltykov. Charming, respected and influential, Catherine certainly considered the count an ideal man to name as father yet it is unlikely that she was telling the truth. Physically Paul resembled Peter and one might safely surmise that Catherine was simply twisting the knife into her husband's memory one more time, choosing a moment when he was too dead to answer back. After all, Catherine's allegations seemed to say, what sort of a man cannot even consummate his own marriage? Certainly not one fit to be Emperor of Russia.

When Catherine gave birth to a daughter by another lover in 1757, relations between the spouses were so strained that Peter shunned the newborn completely. His wife seemed little concerned when her husband packed away his playthings to take mistresses of his own. His eccentric behaviour only made Catherine more popular among courtiers who found him increasingly difficult to deal with. Peter's fatal error was to underestimate the depths of his wife's ambition though, as well as the loyalty and guile of the man she would choose to help her realize the dreams she secretly nursed. Catherine did not only seek passion in the bedroom… she longed for power in the throne room too.

Saltykov, the so-called father of Paul, was not Catherine's only lover and this most physical of ladies enthusiastically took any number of men to her bed. Those who remained loyal were richly rewarded and few were more steadfast that Grigory Orlov, with whom she would conspire to remove her husband from the Russian throne. The couple made no effort to conceal their affair and even had an illegitimate son together, Count Aleksey. Born in 1762, he lived until 1813.

Peter had not been the emperor for long when Catherine and Orlov made their move. The fledgling empress had spent years encouraging factions and building influence at court, winning supporters and undermining her husband. Her efforts came to fruition in late June 1762 when the planned coup was put into action and Peter was arrested. With little choice if he wanted to save himself a potentially nasty fate, he abdicated. When he was reported dead just weeks later, rumours quite understandably flew, but if Catherine knew anything about his demise, she wisely chose not to say so in her memoirs.

Catherine rewarded Orlov with titles and power and trusted his judgement without question, seeing him as her closest advisor. However, her favourite made powerful enemies and for years they dripped poison into Catherine's ear until, tiring of reports of his infidelity, Catherine set Orlov aside whilst he was on diplomatic business and replaced him with Alexander Vasilchikov. This was to become something of a habit for the empress who made a fine art of dispatching one lover on business and moving in his successor whilst her current beau was away. Money, influence and territory awaited the old flames on their return and they generally shrugged pragmatically and got on with life as one more ex of the empress.

More than fifteen years his lover's junior, the romantic and loving Vasilchikov never really stood a chance as anything other than a short-term distraction. Catherine lavished him with money and gifts yet he was unsatisfied, wishing for more than indulgence and money. However, if Catherine had taken Orlov into her confidence and shared with him the most important matters of state, Vasilchikov was no more than a fling. He might wish for power and influence but he was to have no such thing and this refusal to simply go with the flow meant that he was not long for Catherine's bed.

Just as she had sent Orlov on business and installed Vasilchikov in her bed, so too did Catherine dispatch Vasilchikov once he had bored her and, during his absence in 1774, she replaced him with her latest fancy. The newest flame was Grigory Potemkin, a courtier and military leader ten years her junior who was admired widely for his ready charm and intelligence.

In the worldly Potemkin, Catherine saw all that she wanted in a lover, delighting in his attentions at court. However, others saw only a man of low manners, uncouth and common and entirely unsuited to be consort to a woman as powerful as the empress. Of course, Catherine was always mistress of her own destiny and her relationship with Potemkin was passionate, fiery and enduring.

Historians disagree on whether Catherine secretly married Potemkin but for all its fire, their relationship was surprisingly short-lived, with his political influence far outlasting his tenure in the royal bedchamber. Within twelve short months the blazing passion was showing signs of burning out, and whilst Potemkin rose through the ranks of Russian government at a breathtaking speed, Catherine's attraction to him was dimming equally swiftly. As routine dictated, a diplomatic mission was planned for the former favourite and by the time Potemkin returned, Catherine's secretary, Pyotr Zavadovsky, was sharing her bed.

Potemkin seemed anything but disappointed to lose his coveted place at the side of the empress and though their sexual relationship was over, the couple remained close friends. In fact, as Catherine sought new candidates to join the long list of her lovers, she relied upon Potemkin to advise on whether a planned conquest was suitable or not. Court gossips whispered that, on lonely nights, the former lovers occasionally found their way to one another's beds, enjoying the odd liaison for old time's sake.

The affair with Zavadovsky was yet another short fling, any chance for deepening affection marred by Catherine's continuing reliance on Potemkin. Unable to hold his lover's interest, Zavadovsky was usurped for a short time by military hero, Semyon Zorich, and then by Ivan Rimsky-Korsakov, an associate of Potemkin. However, this was to prove an unhappy tryst for all concerned as Catherine, much to her former lover's dismay, became rather too fond of the 23-year-old Rimsky-Korsakov. By now in her mid-forties, Catherine loved to be entertained by the singing and violin playing of the young man, delighting in his attractive and artistic company, whilst Rimsky-Korsakov likewise thrilled at the influence his new lover provided. Still, he made a serious error when he allowed his roving eye to be caught by a lady named Praskovja Bruce.

Bruce was a married lady-in-waiting and friend of Catherine and rumour had it that she auditioned Catherine's lovers once they were chosen by Potemkin. Whether or not this is true, Bruce certainly enjoyed a close association with Potemkin, yet it was not half as close as her association with Rimsky-Korsakov. That particular relationship went far beyond acquaintances and ended up in the bedroom which, as far as Catherine was concerned, was altogether too far. Looking on, Potemkin thought that Bruce and Rimsky-Korsakov's relationship would be nothing but trouble and decided that it was time to say goodbye to both of them.

As Bruce and Rimsky-Korsakov enjoyed a secret assignation, Potemkin ensured that Catherine was directed right into the room in which they were secreted. Having witnessed the betrayal of both her retainer and lover firsthand, Catherine was furious. Despite Rimsky-Korsakov's pleas for clemency the pair were exiled and left St Petersburg together. However, their romance was not to last and Bruce reconciled with her husband, though her position at court was lost to her forever.

After Rimsky-Korsakov, there followed a procession of short-term lovers and it might come as a surprise to learn that, even in her late fifties and with so many affairs behind her, Catherine could still find herself cut by a romantic betrayal. That unhappy experience came courtesy of Potemkin's protege, Alexander Dmitriev-Mamonov, who was in his mid-twenties when he became Catherine's latest attendant. He found his older lover just a little dull, looking to younger ladies to satisfy him in ways that she could not. When word reached Catherine that he was engaged in a liaison with her teenage lady-in-waiting, the empress was sorely wounded but perhaps she was a romantic at heart because she did eventually thaw towards the couple and even gave their marriage her blessing. It is ironic, then, to learn that Mamonov was no sooner married and in Moscow than he began to pine once more for his monarchical former lover, though he never returned to her side.

Finally, at the age of 60, Catherine took to her bed the 22-year-old Platon Zubov, a distant relative of her former favourite, Saltykov. Despite the disparity in age, Catherine fell hard for the young man and he rose swiftly through the ranks at court, becoming the last Russian to be awarded the title of Prince of the Holy Roman Empire.

Zubov was the last lover of Catherine the Great. She died in 1796 after a life lived to the full and without equine interference!

The Wanton Widow

In her lifetime, Augusta of Saxe-Gotha was many things to many people. She was the shy, teenage Princess of Wales, a loving wife, the mother of a king, the 'Wanton Widow' of caricature and a woman so loathed that her funeral cortege was jeered and spat at by the British public who had come to despise her very name. What happened to transform her so thoroughly in the popular opinion and what part did John Stuart, 3rd Earl of Bute, play in the downfall of the widowed Princess of Wales?

Princess Augusta was born to a life of privilege as the daughter of Frederick II, Duke of Saxe-Gotha-Altenburg and Magdalena Augusta of Anhalt-Zerbst. That she would make a dynastic marriage was never in doubt and at the age of 16, the reserved young lady set foot on English shores to begin a new life as the bride of Frederick, Prince of Wales, son of George II and Queen Caroline. Thirteen years her senior, he was already engaged in a war of attrition with his parents, but this is not a tale of an unhappy couple. In fact, it would prove to be quite the opposite…

After a lavish ceremony on 27 April 1736, the new couple embarked on a happy marriage, with Augusta unwavering in her support for her husband throughout his many disputes with his parents. However, when the apparently unassuming, naive Augusta was left a pregnant widow with eight children to raise in 1751, she threw herself on the sympathy of her bereaved father-in-law despite his earlier quarrels with her late husband. To his credit, the king rallied to support his daughter-in-law and her children, one of whom was destined to rule as King George III.

Whilst the death of Frederick left Augusta bereft, she still enjoyed the support of the English people. They admired her devotion to her children and looked on approvingly as she nursed her burgeoning relationship with her parents-in-law. But it was that same devotion to her children that would cause Augusta to take a step from which her reputation would never recover.

Without a father to guide him, Augusta found herself concerned for her young son, George, and took the fateful decision to find a friend and tutor who might steer the young prince on his way to the throne. The man she chose had been introduced to the princess several years before her husband's death when she and her party took shelter from the rain in a picnic tent at Egham races. As the time passed, the group decided to play whist and for that, they needed one more player. The chosen gentleman was none other than the aforementioned John Stuart, 3rd Earl of Bute. This was the start of a friendship with Frederick that lasted until his death and when Augusta was looking for a tutor for her son, the respectable Bute seemed the perfect candidate.

In fact, the quiet young man and the stern earl proved an excellent match; as the future king applied himself to his lessons, he seemed to find an encouraging influence in his unlikely friend. To the people of Britain, however, this was all far from ideal. As far as they were concerned, the widowed Augusta and Bute were far too close for comfort and his influence over the boy was absolute, coming as it did before all other members of the royal household. This included his grandfather, not to mention the uncle who Augusta could not bring herself to trust, seeing in them far too much self-serving ambition. It soon appeared to onlookers that the dowager princess had simply replaced her son's father with Bute and, they whispered, what other duties might he be fulfilling for the widow?

Contemporary rumours that Bute and Augusta were lovers were unfounded yet widespread and to this day, no evidence has been found to prove that their relationship was anything but platonic. This didn't stop the pamphleteers and caricaturists from depicting the pair as wanton and wicked and the reputation stuck, leading to some most unseemly gossip when Bute became prime minister in 1762, during the reign of his former charge. His appointment, it was whispered, could only be down to the services he had rendered to Augusta, who had told her son that he must repay her favourite with this highest of offices.

Whilst there is no doubt that George certainly held his long-time advisor in high regard and was more than happy to support him as prime minister, to suggest that this was to repay sexual favours offered to his mother is spurious. Nevertheless, the juicy gossip reared its head in print when radical Member of Parliament and journalist John Wilkes famously savaged Augusta and Bute in his newspaper, *The North Briton*.

For all of the mockery and rumours that pursued Bute and Augusta, their friendship remained to the last. When the dowager princess died at the age of just 52, Bute mourned her passing keenly. However, even in death, Augusta was not allowed to rest peacefully. At her funeral her coffin was heckled and spat upon in one final insult from the public that had once adored her above all others.

A Prussian Soap Opera

Frederick William II of Prussia was not, perhaps, the most trustworthy of spouses and his conduct caused more than a little difficulty to this particular chronicler of the eighteenth century. After all, how does one categorize the man whose life encompassed multiple infidelities, illegitimate pregnancy, secret abortion, divorce and bigamy? There was just so much drama that this section devoted to scandal seemed to be the only place for Frederick William, who lived through all the excitement and unlikely thrills of the most lurid sort of soap opera.

Born in 1744, Crown Prince Frederick William was a handsome man and, more importantly, a highly eligible one. So bright were his prospects that when his cousin, Elisabeth Christine of Brunswick-Lüneburg, heard that she was to marry him, the young woman must have had high hopes for her future. The politically astute marriage would join the houses of Brunswick-Bevern and Hohenzollern too, yet any optimism the parties felt at the start was soon to be dashed beneath Frederick William's self-indulgent boot.

When he and Elisabeth Christine married in 1765 they were 20 and 19 respectively. The marriage was undoubtedly a good dynastic match for the bride whilst for the groom, a respectable wife in the marriage bed at least went some way to guaranteeing an heir. Rakish and decadent, Frederick William had no intention whatsoever of giving up his high-rolling lifestyle just because he happened to now have a wife. Like our own Hanovers, one of the Crown Prince's favourite pastimes was enjoying the company of actresses and other women of less than ideal repute; marriage or not, this was one hobby he simply was not going to leave behind.

In even the most disastrous royal marriages there is usually the semblance of a honeymoon period, but not for our unlucky couple. Almost immediately after his vows had left his lips, the crown prince was back to his old self, entertaining the ladies at court with his charming and, it must be said, incorrigible ways. Although the newlyweds managed to stand one another just long enough for the crown princess to fall pregnant, when she gave birth to a daughter rather than a son, what little interest Frederick William had in Elisabeth evaporated altogether. That little girl, Princess Frederica Charlotte of Prussia, would go on marry Prince Frederick, Duke of York and

Albany, and become the daughter-in-law of King George III but for now, her birth was simply one more nail in the coffin of a dying marriage.

Perhaps inevitably antipathy turned into loathing and with Frederick William occupied with his own conquests, Elisabeth looked for a little excitement of her own. Young, attractive and vibrant, the crown princess was no longer willing to be neglected and she followed her husband's example with fateful results. It was no secret that that couple were no longer sharing a bed so when Elisabeth fell pregnant, the court erupted into scandal. The father of the child was a court musician named Pietro with whom Elisabeth intended to elope but when her lover was arrested and executed, Elisabeth's pregnancy mysteriously ended. In his memoirs, Baron Gijsbert Jan van Hardenbroek claimed that the unhappy young woman procured herbs with which to terminate her pregnancy. Whether this is true we cannot know but it is certainly not an impossibility and, faced with the irrefutable proof of his wife's betrayal, her hypocritical husband turned to his uncle, Frederick the Great, and asked him to intervene.

That intervention was swift, stern and merciless. Frederick had Elisabeth placed under house arrest and in April 1769 the royal marriage was annulled on the grounds of adultery. Still only 22 years old, Elisabeth was not released from her gilded prison and never saw her daughter again, surely the most devastating punishment that could be meted out. The crown princess lived on into her nineties and, like George I's wife, Sophia Dorothea of Celle, never regained her freedom. She lived a lonely and secluded life of perpetual disgrace whilst her former husband was free to cavort and rabble-rouse to his heart's content.

In the year that his marriage collapsed, Frederick William happily began an affair that would outlast all of his other relationships, continuing for nearly three decades. The lady in question was Wilhelmine Enke, the 16-year-old daughter of a court musician, and Frederick William was crazy about her. Installed as his official mistress, she was mother to five children by her noble lover. For Frederick the Great, however, whilst Wilhelmine might make a fine mistress for his flighty young nephew, she was no substitute for the real thing. In fact, before the annulment was even final, he was already urging Frederick William to look around for the next dynastic match.

That questionable honour fell to Frederika Louisa of Hesse-Darmstadt who was just 18 when she married Frederick William, the ceremony taking place three months after the annulment of his first marriage. Once again the union was not happy as the groom continued his extra-marital assignations with Wilhelmine and any number of other willing ladies. This time, however, Frederick the Great's ambitions for the marriage were fulfilled and Frederika gave birth to seven children by her husband, providing no shortage of heirs. With Frederika there were no rumours of affairs, no illegitimate pregnancies and, best of all for the stability of the house of Hohenzollern, no troublesome musicians in need of execution.

Frederick William and Frederika were crowned king and queen of Prussia on 17 August 1786, and one might be forgiven for thinking that this might be an ideal place for a happy ending. However, if that were the case then the king's place here in our rundown of court scandals would be misplaced. Besides, that would mean Frederick William, by now a king with plenty besides affairs of the heart to occupy him had finally learned the meaning of self-control, and there was no chance of that.

Although the marriage of king and queen was somewhat lacking in affection, there was one thing in Frederika's chambers that her husband was very fond of. It wasn't her sense of humour, her intelligence or even her looks… it was her lady-in-waiting and his affair with Julie von Voss resulted in a morganatic, bigamous marriage. All of this whilst running a country, being a husband and maintaining his official mistress.

When Julie died in 1789, her job as lady-in-waiting was taken by 21-year-old Sophie von Dönhoff. You will not be surprised to learn that it wasn't the only role vacated by Julie that Sophie would take. True to form, Frederick William married Sophie too, the last nuptial act in a scandalous life.

You Can't Choose Your Parents…

The royal families of the eighteenth century were not, to put it mildly, the most stable of domestic environments. With lies, affairs and intrigue the fuel on which courts thrived and little chance of privacy for those who wore the crown, it was not always relationships between husbands and wives that broke down. Whilst Frederick, Prince of Wales, enjoyed a happy marriage to Augusta of Saxe-Gotha, his relationship with his parents was the stuff of pure, unadulterated melodrama.

Frederick was born in Hanover in 1707 as the son of the future George II and Caroline of Ansbach. When the little boy was just 7 years old his parents left him in the care of his great-uncle and travelled for England, where the coronation of George I was taking place; he would not see them again for fourteen years. His grandfather George I wanted Frederick to remain in Hanover as a ceremonial figurehead. Away from his parents, he grew into a supremely confident young man. Frederick was no shrinking violet and his life in Europe was lived to the full, with plenty of partying providing the counterpoint to the official duties he was required to perform in his father's absence.

In something of a romantic haze, when Frederick heard that his father was in talks to marry him off to Wilhelmine of Prussia, he was most taken with the idea. Frustrated that his parents were deliberately delaying the matter, the impetuous young man took matters into his own hands and sent word to the Prussian court of his desire, a shocking breach of royal marriage protocol. This wilful act sealed his fate, and the king demanded that Frederick leave Hanover and join him in England, where he might better be able to keep an eye on his troublesome son

The last thing Frederick wanted was to find himself under the scrutiny of parents who he no longer really knew, nor did he wish to move to a country where he would be known as the Prince of Wales. Still, Frederick obeyed the wishes of his father and made the journey to England with absolutely *no* intention of becoming a dutiful son. Upon his arrival he threw himself into his new life with admirable gusto and was soon making influential friends at court, though his relationship with his parents was understandably distant from the start. During his time away from the family, Frederick had acquired new siblings and one of them, Prince William, Duke of Cumberland, was unapologetically the favourite of the king and queen, which cannot have brought any joy to the young Prince of Wales. Politically opposed to many of his father's ideals, Frederick instead found a kindred spirit in the waspish and indiscrete Baron John Hervey. Whether Frederick and the bisexual Hervey were lovers has never been proven but regardless of the nature of their relationship, their friendship was intense.

That friendship ended in 1732 when Anne Vane, who was mistress to both baron and prince as well as lady-in-waiting to Queen Caroline, gave birth to a son, FitzFrederick Cornwall Vane. With the paternity of the child in doubt, the two men grew swiftly apart. Despite the uncertainty as to who was actually responsible for the boy, the already debt-ridden prince continued to plough money into Anne's household, regardless of the queen's firm belief that the child's father was none other than her own favourite, Hervey.

Following Frederick's marriage to Augusta of Saxe-Gotha in 1736, it seemed that the prince might finally be able to find something approaching contentment. He continued to spend as though money was no object and though his continued requests for cash from the king were always met with a refusal, this did nothing to deter him. He continued to arouse his father's ire by making unapologetic ties with opposition politicians and when the king failed to return as expected from a trip to Hanover in 1737, his son's behaviour proved very telling.

Rumours spread that the king had been lost at sea, presumed drowned. The court buzzed with gossip and the queen was beside herself with anxiety, yet the young prince seemed almost excited at the prospect of finally becoming king in place of the man with whom he had so little in common. In fact, Frederick's ambitions were to be frustrated when George appeared in England very much alive, if afflicted with painful piles. When the king took to his bed, the Prince of Wales stirred up court gossip that his father was on the brink of death to such a degree that the ill man was forced to make a personal appearance simply to prove that he was far from the grave.

This mischievous bit of gossip-mongering did no favours to the relationship between the king and prince and, when the young man needed money yet again, he didn't even bother approaching his father. Instead, Frederick went straight to Parliament and successfully achieved an increase in his allowance, much to the annoyance of George. So fractured was their relationship that the king began to look into the legality of schemes that would split the succession, ensuring that his favourite son might rule in Britain whilst Frederick would assume only the throne of Hanover.

Just as the birth of the tragically short-lived George William caused strife between George II and his father, it was a birth that provided the final push to splinter the relationship between Frederick and George II. When Augusta fell pregnant, the implications of a son were all too clear; should the unborn child be a boy, then William would slip out of his place as second in line to the throne in favour of Frederick's own son.

Frederick, meanwhile, was determined that his wife would not give birth to their first child beneath his father's roof. Instead, when Augusta went into labour in July 1737, he actually convinced the unfortunate woman to leave Hampton Court undercover of night and took her to St James's Palace, with Queen Caroline in hot pursuit. This was a blatant breach of accepted royal protocol, as members of the family and senior courtiers normally witnessed a royal birth.

The queen arrived to find herself already a grandmother, with Augusta having given birth to a daughter. It was a slight from which the queen was never to recover and she died later that same year, having never reconciled with Frederick. Though he had attempted to visit during her final days, the king refused him admittance to his mother's sickroom, still unable to forgive him.

Just as his father had been, so too was Frederick banished from court, instead establishing an alternative court at Leicester House. Here opposition colleagues and a flamboyant social circle gathered, much to the king's disapproval.

A final coda to the story is one that proves the pointlessness of the king's plans to try and split the crowns. Frederick died in 1751, predeceasing George II by almost a decade and rendering succession concerns moot. The bereaved father chose not to attend the low-key funeral of his unfortunate son, putting a final, heartless full stop to their fractious relationship.

The Many Lovers of the King of Bling

When it comes to the kings of Georgian Britain, one alone has come to embody the decadence, glamour and largesse of the era. For George, Prince of Wales, Prince Regent and, eventually, King George IV of the United Kingdom, scandal was simply part of life. The adventures of his estranged wife, Caroline of Brunswick are investigated elsewhere in this volume but for now, the stage belongs alone to this shamelessly scandalous gentleman. Buried in debt, distracted by fancies and living his privileged life to the full,

George had dozens of lovers and mistresses during his life and it is time to meet just a few of them.

Before we plunge into the chequered personal life of George, a little insight into his personality might help us to understand how it was that he succeeded in winning so many women to his side. Naturally, being the heir to the throne did no harm, but George has been remembered, perhaps unfairly, for his love of gold and ostentation, the enormous corsets that confined his bulk in his later years and the father for whom he served as regent, mad King George III.

'If there was ever a monarch formed for personal popularity, that monarch was George IV; showy in his habits, and elegant in his manners, the consciousness of the highest rank had only made him the first gentleman of England. A man of talents unusual on a throne, a man of accomplishment, handsome in his person, and polished in his tastes, he had every qualification for popularity.'[21]

As *Blackwoods Edinburgh Magazine* testified, George was a man of good looks and great charm, of breeding and education and his taste was often unquestionably good, if given to extravagance. Highly intelligent, he had a weakness for personal indulgence and keeping up with his continental crowned peers, and when he turned 18, this desire for lavishness leapt to the fore. Unlike their son, George's parents, George III and Charlotte of Mecklenburg-Strelitz, lived a quiet and contented life. Not for them the ceremony and pomp of monarchy, the scandal and excitement that had touched the lives of so many of our royal characters. George III was remarkable amongst the Hanoverian kings of Britain in that he never took a mistress, and was content in the company of his loving wife, but his heir would more than make up for that.

As soon as he was able, George threw off the restrictions of parental authority and went a little wild. Like so many young men and women have before and since, he revelled in his new found freedom and was soon spending money as though it was no object. He partied, gambled and enjoyed the company of beautiful women so, when he took himself off for a family visit to the theatre in 1779, fate was waiting to stick its troublesome oar in.

The show was *The Winter's Tale* and in the leading role of Perdita was 22-year-old Mary Darby Robinson, daughter of a naval captain and sometime schoolmistress. Abandoned by her father in infancy and raised by her go-getting and resolute mother, the actress had lived a wildly eventful life. Mary was tutored in the arts of the stage by no less a man than David Garrick himself, who saw in the girl a great talent just waiting to be nurtured. Under his tutelage she thrived, earning a place opposite the great Shakespearean in *King Lear*. It was an amazing opportunity and for a time, Mary seemed destined for the highest echelons of the theatre.

As it so often would though, fate had other plans in store for the young lady and Mary's career trajectory was shattered by smallpox. To the rescue rode a lowly yet gentlemanly clerk named Thomas Robinson, with whom Mary's mother was most enamoured, seeing in him a perfect husband for the teenage actress. Encouraged by her mother, she accepted Robinson's hand and set aside her dreams of a career in the theatre in deference to a life as a wife. However, the seemingly unassuming clerk was hiding a secret that George might well have sympathized with: he liked the high life but lacked the income to live it. Whilst the Prince of Wales could turn to Parliament and his father for help, Thomas Robinson had no such resources to fall back on.

With no prospects or inheritance, the couple struggled on unhappily and when Mary, her husband and their infant daughter were placed in a debtor's prison, she decided that the time had come to wrest back control of her life. Though she remained with her husband upon his release, Mary was no longer content to let him ruin the family and returned to her true passion, acting.

Mary went back to the theatre with a vengeance as Juliet in 1776; she was a hit, winning the hearts of her audience and the acclaim of critics. With her star rising high, she was thrilled to win the role of Perdita and London buzzed with word of her breathtaking talent and beauty, chatter that would no doubt have reached the ears of the 17-year-old Prince of Wales. A lover of beauty and women in equal measure, the young man fell head over heels for the lady on stage and began writing her breathless love notes, addressed to Perdita from Florizel.

Mary, of course, was far from a blushing innocent and was well used to stage door Johnnies declaring their undying affection. She resisted the prince's approach at first but once she agreed to meet him in person, the stage was set for a most passionate assignation. The attraction was mutual and intense and when George recklessly offered Mary £20,000 if she would leave her husband and career behind to become his mistress, she accepted.

It was a fatal error.

As we have seen from George's tireless pursuit of Maria Fitzherbert, there was little he found more irresistible than a woman who appeared to be playing hard to get. As soon as Mary accepted the role of official, maintained mistress, the prince's ardour cooled. The affair limped along for some time but it soon appeared that Mary had gone from one bad situation to another and once again, it was her career that took the brunt.

In 1781, George decided that he did not like Mary half as much as he had initially thought. Rather than let her down gently he simply cut off all contact and the promised £20,000 was nowhere to be seen. The Georgian press, never the kindest era of the fourth estate, were merciless in their mockery of the unfortunate woman, commenting 'Florizel' now neglects her for one old enough to be a mother to both'[22] and later, with tongue firmly in cheek, *The Morning Herald and Daily Advertiser* sneered with barely-concealed delight:

'*Perdita* finding all arts and devices fail in attempting the recovery of the *inconstant Florizel*, has at length abandoned the pursuit, and is now certainly preparing for her re-entry on the stage, with a view, no doubt of ensnaring another *princely heart*, on its first enlargement from the *royal nursery!*'[23]

In fact the press was mistaken. Fearing a backlash due to her highly-publicized relationship with the prince, Mary instead withdrew from public life and as her debts mounted, devoted herself to trying to secure her £20,000. Despite efforts on her behalf by senior political figures the money resolutely failed to materialize and Mary eventually accepted £5000 and an annual income of £500. Still only in her twenties, the unfortunate and spurned woman attempted to distance herself from the scandal as George simply moved on without a care, already looking for his next amour.

He settled on Elizabeth Armistead, a friend and future wife of Charles James Fox, who enchanted George when he saw her about town. However, Elizabeth's tastes were even more expensive than George's and it was she who cooled on him, going off to see the continent once his charms no longer interested her.

George enjoyed a short, uncharacteristically subtle liaison with Grace Dalrymple Elliott and when Grace claimed that her daughter, Georgina, was his child, the prince would hear none of it. Instead, he was happy to encourage those who pointed the accusing figure at her long-time lover, the Marquess of Cholmondeley. Although far from the only candidate, Lord Cholmondeley raised the little girl as his own and George, still only a tender 20 years of age, skipped away once more, free to continue his self-indulgent life.

In 1783 the prince reached the age of 21 and found himself in receipt of a parliamentary grant of £60,000. For a man with a love of spending this was a dream come true and as his parents looked on in helpless horror, George raced through his income without a care in the world. That same year his eye was taken by the 30-year-old Frances Villiers, Countess of Jersey, but Lady Jersey resisted his dubious attractions for a decade, perfectly happy with the several lovers she already had. Unbowed, he transferred his attention to a short liaison with Elizabeth Lamb, Viscountess Melbourne, though the grandest of his grand passions waited on the horizon.

Eventually, the prince met Maria Fitzherbert and, and as we saw in our chapter on royal marriages, this was a relationship that would far outlast his infatuation with Mary Robinson. The couple were married in 1785 but that was not the end for George's voyages into the unchartered ocean of romance. Indeed, now George was occupied with his Maria, Lady Jersey suddenly began to thaw, tempting him away from his secret wife's bosom.

A surprising favourite of Queen Charlotte, the cunning and manipulative Lady Jersey enjoyed no small amount of influence and was an inveterate social climber. Her reputation as a woman who liked the company of men was known to all except her trusting husband, George Bussy Villiers, the 4th Earl of Jersey, who was Gentleman of the Bedchamber to George III. Known for her beauty, Lady Jersey certainly had her enemies thanks to her propensity for gossip and, it must be said, making trouble. Away from the bedchamber, political discussions were taking place that would play right into Lady Jersey's hands as, after a decade of marriage to Maria Fitzherbert, a royal wedding loomed.

The gossip of a secret marriage to Mrs Fitzherbert had gathered so much traction that Charles James Fox denied the rumours in parliament and after years of financially bailing out their son whilst he gave them nothing in return, in 1794 George and Charlotte finally tightened their purse strings.

The king gave his son an ultimatum that he could not fail to accept: if he wished for any more handouts, he must marry his cousin, Princess Caroline of Brunswick. By now his mistress, Lady Jersey encouraged George to accept the hand of Caroline, sure that this unwanted wife would be no match for her own attractions and would displace Maria Fitzherbert once and for all. When he did marry, Lady Jersey was given the position of Lady of the Bedchamber and devoted herself to making Caroline's life miserable.

Making no secret of her relationship with the prince, Lady Jersey mocked his new bride's dress, looks and manners. The public and caricaturists, however, found Lady Jersey's lack of discretion distasteful and Caroline's quiet acceptance of her husband's bad behaviour only served to increase her own popularity. The press was happy to draw attention to Lady Jersey's position in the prince's life, with *True Briton* sniffily commenting in 1797:

'Lady JERSEY might be expected to have more policy, to say nothing of virtue, delicacy and higher motives, than to appear in the PRINCE OF WALES'S box, after all that has been said in the *Scandalous Chronicle*. The Public would doubtless feel a high gratification in seeing an illustrious Female, who has a proper title to the box, appear in it; and they must suffer a painful emotion every time they behold the place occupied as it has *lately been*.'[24]

Lady Jersey resigned her role and though the affair limped on for a little longer, by 1799, it was over. Lady Jersey did not go quietly and harangued her former lover for years but all to no avail as the woman he furiously called an 'infernal jezebel' was resigned to the past along with Mary, Maria, Grace and even his wife.

The lady who did the most to help George forget his supposedly adored Maria Fitzherbert was Isabella Ingram-Seymour-Conway, Marchioness of Hertford and wife of Francis Ingram-Seymour-Conway, 2nd Marquess of Hertford. George met her in 1807 and befriended her Tory husband, insinuating himself into the Hertford household and the affections of the

48-year-old Lady Hertford. Indeed, whenever she was out of town, Keeper of the Privy Purse, Benjamin Bloomfield confided that George descended into a depression so deep that the prince was driven to unreachable distraction.

Lady Hertford indulged the prince's fancies and was an intellectual sounding board, happy to discuss the politics and affairs of the day. Some historians have concluded that the pair's bond went far deeper than the physical and that they were possibly not even sexually intimate at all. Whether or not they shared a bed, the couple certainly enjoyed a deep and intense emotional attachment and when George became Prince Regent in 1811, Lady Hertford enjoyed considerable influence.

George's affection for Lady Hertford waned, as all of George's affections did in time, when he laid eyes on the woman who became his next and final fancy. In 1819, whilst keeping Lady Hertford dangling on one arm, on the other he took his last lover Elizabeth, Lady Conyngham. Although he had preferred older ladies in his youth, Lady Conyngham was fifty, seven years George's junior. For a year he juggled the affections of Lady Conyngham and Lady Hertford but the writing was on the wall and Conyngham soon supplanted her rival just as Hertford had supplanted Fitzherbert. Never let it be said, after all, that George wasn't predictable in his waxing and waning fancies.

By the time George succeeded as king in 1820, he and Lady Conyngham were inseparable. It seemed that, in his later years, George had finally learned the value of discretion or, more likely, the very married Lady Conyngham recognized the importance of not inflaming the public opinion as Lady Jersey had done so many years earlier. The couple wisely kept a low profile as Caroline of Brunswick pursued her divorce yet the marchioness played her advantage to the hilt, advancing her husband's rank and her own alongside it, along the way securing several appointments that benefitted her spouse and favourites too.

Lady Conyngham became a permanent fixture around the king and she wielded huge domestic power. Flitting in and out of Carlton House unseen, wherever the king went his lover was never far away. She was there at the coronation from which the queen was turned away, happened to visit the theatre on the evenings George attended and, on the day after the king died at Windsor, it was she who left the castle. With his lover there to the bitter end, George had achieved something he had perhaps always sought: he had never, in truth, been alone.

For all his mistresses and his disastrous marriage, George acquired women with the same rapaciousness he acquired clothes, carriages, gold and silverware and, crucially, debt. It was as though the man once known as Prinny simply could never be satisfied. He won the woman he adored and immediately she lost her shine, sending him spinning headlong into the next affair, and every new lover, was the one. In truth, perhaps George never found his true love or perhaps she was, in fact, that Catholic widow he had married in Mayfair; perhaps even the man himself never really knew, and could never stop searching for an ideal that was forever just out of reach.

A Duchess, a Duke… and His Best Friend

In the early days of the 1770s, all of European nobility marshalled their most eligible daughters, summoned the dressmakers, the etiquette experts and the portrait painters and welcomed the news that Catherine the Great was searching for a bride for her 18-year-old son, Grand Duke Paul. The hand of the young man would be a fine prize for any royal house although the successful candidate would also have to deal with Catherine, whose relationship with her son was fractured to say the least. The heir to the throne of Russia had been raised first by his paternal aunt and then, after her death, by any number of other carers whilst Catherine was employed in the business of ruling the country. Regardless of her feelings for her son, Catherine certainly did care for one thing and that was the future of the house of Romanov. It was time, she decided, for Paul to marry, and the choice of bride would be made by Catherine.

When news reached the Hesse-Darmstadt court in Prenzlau that Paul was up for grabs, the ears of the Landgrave certainly perked up. Louis IX and his wife, Caroline of Zweibrücken, had raised their three daughters to be the perfect candidates for such a role and all were placed on the coveted shortlist. Aged 16, 18 and 19 respectively, Louise, Wilhelmina and Amalie were all likely matches for Paul. Through to the second round of marital auditions, the trio was called to Russia for an audience with the empress but before they went, all three were put through a crash refresher course in courtly behaviour.

The stakes for the young ladies could not have been higher; dressed to impress and the very image of demure, dignified future brides, the girls were dispatched for Russia and their chance to join Hesse-Darmstadt to one of the most powerful houses of the era. The ship on which they travelled was captained by Grand Duke Paul's best friend, Count Andrey Razumovsky, the nephew of the 'Night Emperor'. Charming, cultured and attractive, he proved diverting company to the trio of young ladies and one of the girls in particular took a shine to the worldly gentleman. Impressed by what she saw, Wilhelmina's initial friendship with Razumovsky was the start of a road that led to romantic intrigue.

Just 48 hours after meeting the three sisters in St Petersburg, Paul made his choice and declared that he wished to marry Wilhelmina. Catherine heartily approved of the choice, finding her future daughter-in-law to be a perfect candidate, and the wheels began to turn. Although they missed out on the Russian prize, Louise and Amalie would go on to make dynastic matches of their own but for now, the happy ending appeared to belong to Wilhelmina. She and the Grand Duke were married in an enormous wedding ceremony by the Russian Orthodox Church on 29 September 1773 and Wilhelmina, now named Natalia Alexeievna, took the title of Grand Duchess.

From the start, the bright and bubbly new bride enjoyed immense popularity in St Petersburg where, since the empress liked her, everybody dutifully followed suit and proclaimed her perfect. This honeymoon period was destined not to last and to Catherine's horror, it eventually became apparent that the grand duchess was anything but an innocent, dutiful wife. Instead the girl who had seemed so demure was highly ambitious on behalf of her husband and schemed to put him on the throne regardless of what his mother's plans might be.

Although the newly-renamed Natalia's professional ambitions might rest with her spouse, her affections were elsewhere and she was soon embroiled in a love affair with Andrey Razumovsky, the man who had squired her on that fateful first visit. Known as an inveterate womanizer, Razumovsky was Paul's close friend and just as the two men shared most things, they eventually shared Natalia too. The couple made little effort to conceal their relationship and were soon the talk of the court, though Paul somehow remained blissfully or, perhaps, wilfully unaware of exactly what was going on right under his royal nose. The worldly Catherine saw all too clearly how things were going though and determined to put a stop to it. It was a bittersweet irony then, that when Paul became aware of his mother's efforts to exile Razumovsky, he intervened to ensure his friend could remain at court. A touching show of devotion between pals, to be sure, but it also demonstrates just how blind Paul was to the actions of his wife and best friend.

When news emerged of Natalia's pregnancy in 1775, more than a few eyebrows were raised on the matter of paternity. One might imagine that Catherine would take the opportunity to rid herself of her troublesome daughter-in-law but instead, the empress took a far more prosaic view. The child, to all intents and purposes, was a valuable commodity and so long as everyone held their nerve, could be happily explained away as the official heir to the throne of Russia. It was hardly a situation Catherine wanted to disrupt so regardless of what the gossips might whisper, if the baby was a boy, then it would be proclaimed the son of Paul and heir to the crown. In another ironic twist that the pragmatic empress no doubt appreciated, she had been given the same get-out clause when she fell pregnant during her own affair many years earlier with Count Sergei Saltykov.

In any event, Catherine had no need to worry about the father of this particular child, nor what would become of the royal marriage upon the birth. After suffering a prolonged and agonizing labour, Natalia delivered a stillborn son on 15 April 1776. The hesitation of her doctors to perform a Caesarian proved fatal and when they finally did operate, neither mother nor child stood a chance of survival.

At the loss of his wife, Paul was distraught and for a short time refused to release her body for burial. As we have already learned, however, royal marriage was a business that waited for no man, grieving or not and, five months later, he had married again, much to his mother's relief.

A Necklace Fit for a Queen

Whether a courtier or a king, a queen or an equerry, beneath the glittering chandeliers that illuminated the Palace of Versailles, gossip and intrigue were the currency of the court. Secrets were spilled, scandals were traded and rumour gained traction before the truth could even be whispered. In 1785 this heady hothouse was the stage for an erupting drama that engulfed the Queen of France herself, the flames fed by political point- scoring and growing public unhappiness with monarchy and government. It had all the ingredients to set Versailles alight, with money, gemstones and ambition taking starring roles in the affair of the diamond necklace.

The story begins in 1772 when Louis XV was searching for a unique, extravagant and breathtaking gift for his beloved *maîtresse-en-titre*, Madame du Barry. The lady loved largesse and Louis loved to spend so it came as little surprise when the king hit upon the idea of the finest diamond necklace the world had ever seen. With an eye-watering budget of two million livres, Louis approached the court jewellers, Boehmer and Bassenge, with the commission. A design was conceived consisting of an elaborate necklace that showcased nearly seven hundred diamonds and would be not only a piece of jewellery, but a work of art. The jewellers told the king that such a piece would take years to complete but, determined to honour the commission, set about the job.

In fact, Louis XV died just two years later and left Madame du Barry with no place at Versailles. With her position at court lost, gone were her hopes of taking ownership of the magnificent necklace on which payment was still outstanding. However, Boehmer and Bassenge pointed out that the piece had been commissioned by the house of Bourbon and somebody had to buy it. Perhaps, they suggested to Louis XVI, it might look rather fetching around the slender neck of Marie Antoinette, the new Queen of France and Navarre.

It was a brave gambit but one that was doomed to fail. Whether it was Louis, Marie Antoinette or both who decided that they did not want the necklace, we cannot be sure but, whoever made the decision, the jeweller was informed that there was to be no sale. With the hugely valuable trinket burning a hole in their coffers, Boehmer and Bassenge made other aborted attempts to sell the necklace but every time, they were frustrated in their efforts.

Elsewhere in France, far from the glamour of palaces and necklaces that could bankrupt a small nation, a woman known to some as Jeanne de Saint-Rémy de Valois, to others as Jeanne de la Motte was hatching a plot of her own. The mistress of Louis-René-Édouard de Rohan, the Cardinal de Rohan, she was nothing if not ambitious. Two centuries earlier, high in the distant branches of her family tree, Jeanne could claim Henri de Saint-Rémy, illegitimate son of Henry II, as an ancestor and she was determined to make some use this little bit of noble blood. Although she had grown up in poverty, Jeanne had a keen intelligence and was eager to get what she saw as her due, no matter what it took. Exploiting her Valois name, Jeanne requested and was given an audience with Louis XVI to plead her case. Her tale fell on sympathetic ears and she was awarded the annuity she requested, her claim to the Valois name recognized. Things were finally going Jeanne's way and for a time, she occupied a position, albeit a lowly one, at court.

Jeanne was not born to be lowly though and eventually she struck out alone, falsely labelling herself a countess and fatefully inveigling herself into the cardinal's life. Rohan had incurred the dislike of Marie Antoinette by passing gossip about the then dauphine back to her mother during his years as ambassador to Vienna and he was keen to find a way back into royal favour. Imagine his excitement then when Jeanne wove an entirely fictional tale of her considerable influence at court, claiming to be particularly well-liked by the queen herself. When the cardinal asked Jeanne to make representations on his behalf she readily agreed and promised that she would deliver correspondence direct to Marie Antoinette.

In fact, Jeanne took the letters only as far as her husband, Nicolas de la Motte, and his friend and former army colleague, Rétaux de Villette. The cunning trio hatched a plot to commit a breathtaking fraud with the cardinal their dupe and to start the ball rolling, Villette crafted responses to Rohan's letters, on which he forged the queen's signature. Neither Jeanne nor Villette knew that in signing the letters as Marie Antoinette de France, the fraudster had actually left a clue to his dishonesty. The queen signed her letters simply Marie Antoinette but, of course, Rohan didn't know this either and for that reason the mistake passed unnoticed. Instead of raising the alarm against the fraudsters, the unwitting cardinal was thrilled to receive kindly missives from the queen whom he now believed had forgiven him. For Jeanne, the correspondence became just one more way to fleece Rohan and in her letters, the queen asked the cardinal to lend her large sums of money, which Jeanne happily pocketed.

Jeanne, however, had far bigger ambitions. So convincing was she when she described her close friendship with Marie Antoinette that Charles Auguste Boehmer, who had been trying to sell the necklace all over Europe, made contact with her. He explained that he had heard of Jeanne's relationship with the queen and wondered whether she might be able to convince her royal friend to take the necklace off his hands. Jeanne readily and helpfully agreed, sure that Rohan was the man who could help make those diamonds hers. For his part, Rohan was so utterly focused on winning his way back into Marie Antoinette's affections that he either truly didn't realize or chose not to recognize that this unorthodox correspondence should have raised his suspicions from the start. Instead, he ventured to ask the 'queen' if she might consent to meet him in person and she replied that she would. In the autumn of 1784, the no doubt delighted Rohan was invited to a nighttime meeting in the fortuitously-named Grove of Venus, deep in the gardens of Versailles. He was warned, however, that the liaison must remain a secret for both their sakes.

Whether Rohan was really fooled or it was a matter of wishful thinking we cannot know. However, when he arrived for his meeting, there was indeed a lady waiting to receive him. Though he believed her to be Marie Antoinette she was actually Nicole Leguay, a prostitute and sometime actress, who was disguised as the queen and playing the role of a lifetime. During their meeting Rohan was delighted to hear that the queen had forgiven his earlier indiscretions, and that he would soon be able to return to his rightful place at court. Immensely grateful to Jeanne for her part in brokering the arrangement, he was happy to hand over even more money to her in the belief that she would pass it along to the queen, who would put it to philanthropic use. In fact, Jeanne spent the cash on living the high life that she so adored, finding that doors opened to her as a monied charmer with spurious royal connections.

Eventually, after a few months of this coming and going and with letters from the queen a regular occurrence, Jeanne put the next stage of her plan into action. In January 1785, the eager to please Rohan received a letter from Marie Antoinette that mentioned the famous necklace. In her correspondence she told Rohan that she longed to own the trinket but, given that she was already unpopular with the people of the country, she could hardly be seen to be making such an extravagant purchase. Perhaps, she ventured, the cardinal might broker the deal for her and speak to the jeweller to negotiate a discrete payment plan, whilst claiming that Rohan himself had bought the necklace to present as a gift. That way Marie Antoinette would get her gift yet would be utterly blameless, the jeweller would be rid of the diamond millstone and the cardinal would more than earn his place in the heart of court life.

Just as Jeanne knew he would, Cardinal de Rohan jumped to do the queen's bidding and approached the jewellers. As proof of his intentions and authority, he showed them the fraudulent letters from Marie Antoinette authorizing the purchase at a price of two million livres, paid in instalments. The deal was struck and Rohan took custody of the necklace. Although he believed that his actions had saved the queen's public face and ensured that she could finally have the necklace she desired, he had actually set in place the foundations for a dreadfully embarrassing affair.

When Rohan arrived at Jeanne's house with the necklace, he was received by a man who Jeanne explained was a member of the royal household, dispatched to collect the bounty. Rohan duly handed the diamond necklace over, little suspecting he had actually passed it to Villette, who then gave it to Jeanne's husband, Nicolas. The necklace was never seen in one piece again, but soon Nicolas was in London, selling off an enormous quantity of diamonds that had been removed from that self-same trinket.

Why Jeanne didn't take the opportunity to flee we cannot be sure, but any unexpected departure would undoubtedly have raised suspicions and as far as Rohan or anyone else knew, she was innocent. However, what didn't appear to raise Rohan's suspicions was the fact that Jeanne suddenly had more money than ever at her disposal and she wasn't shy about spending it. Yet as the due date of the first instalment approached Jeanne must have known that no payment would have been made and when that happened, Boehmer and Bassenge went straight to Marie Antoinette. They explained that Rohan had taken custody of the necklace on her behalf and politely requested the first, now overdue, instalment. Unaware that Rohan was as much a victim of deception as herself, the horrified queen asked her husband to intervene and speak to Rohan. Of course, Louis agreed, keen to settle the matter and his wife's upset once and for all.

Cheered by his new place in Marie Antoinette's affections, on 15 August 1785 the unsuspecting Cardinal de Rohan prepared to officiate before the court and royal family at the Feast of the Assumption, also Marie Antoinette's name day. However, he was summoned to the private quarters of the king and queen and here heard the charges against him from the king's own lips. Desperate to defend himself, Rohan protested that he had been duped and yet offered now to borrow the money to pay for the necklace himself. Louis, however, was keen to follow correct procedure and, mindful of his wife's distress and the damage this could do to an already unpopular monarchy, he had the cardinal arrested and taken to the Bastille, where he would remain for ten months.

With the cardinal's very public removal from the packed Palace of Versailles, the court erupted into excited gossip. As the net tightened Jeanne attempted to flee, but on 18 August she was arrested. In the days that followed, Nicole Leguay, who had posed as the queen in the Grove of Venus, and Rétaux de Villette, the forger, were also arrested and questioned about their part in the affair, with Villette quick to admit that he was the man behind the letters. Nicolas, however, had made good his escape to the safety of England, where he wisely chose to remain.

At their trial, Leguay and Rohan were cleared of any wrongdoing whilst Nicolas was sentenced to life imprisonment in his absence. For Villette and Jeanne, things were not to end happily either. Villette was exiled from France and fled to Italy whilst Jeanne was whipped, branded and sentenced to incarceration for life in the Salpêtrière. Unsurprisingly, her story didn't end there and she escaped her prison within twelve months, dying in London in 1791 in somewhat unusual circumstances.

The whole affair caused enormous scandal and excitement among the people of France but, despite the fact that the queen was neither accused, charged, nor found guilty of any wrongdoing it was she upon whom their most drastic disapproval fell. Her dislike of the cardinal was no secret and for some, the affair of the diamond necklace had been nothing more than Marie Antoinette finally carrying out her long-planned revenge.

Already seen as a woman who never knew when to stop spending, there were some who believed that Marie Antoinette had known exactly what was going on in her supposedly innocent name and had schemed to get her hands on the necklace without anyone realizing she was doing so. To these people, she was the mastermind and instigator of the plot and even those who didn't believe Marie Antoinette was behind the scheme recognized that, by finding Rohan not guilty, the court had implicitly suggested that the queen arranging mysterious midnight assignations was not at all unlikely.

On top of that, Marie Antoinette shouldered the sole blame for the humiliatingly public arrest of the cardinal, with Louis painted as an innocent who was bullied by his wife into becoming an instrument of her spiteful revenge. After all, the king had not given Rohan a chance to make his own case before he was taken to the Bastille and had instead listened to his wife's charges and accusations without even a flicker of doubt. Her case was not helped by the memoirs Jeanne published once she reached the safety of London, where she pointed an unflinching finger at Marie Antoinette. She was an innocent victim in the thrall of the queen, Jeanne wrote passionately, claiming that the de la Mottes were sucked in by the scheming monarch's wicked plots.

The sad affair of the diamond necklace followed Marie Antoinette all the way to the guillotine. To the end of her life she was tarnished as the woman who had schemed against the cardinal, the sort of hussy so lacking in morals that she was happy to meet a man after dark in the palace gardens, defraud him and then have him arrested before the entire court. It was simply one more body blow against the monarchy aimed, as so many were, squarely at Marie Antoinette.

The Princess and the Equerry

We have, on our jaunt through the royal courts of eighteenth century Europe, met plenty of members of the house of Hanover, and this tale of a tragic love affair concerns yet another of the many children of George III and Queen Charlotte. Some of this noble brood lived tragically short lives, some entered scandalous unions and some, including the future George IV, simply did nothing by halves. For most of the royal daughters, however, excitement was a notion that could only be dreamed of – their lives confined to Windsor and the role of companion to their mother. Engaged in caring for her beloved husband and dealing with his fast-failing mental health, Charlotte relied on their companionship and kept the girls closer than they might wish to be, not quite willing to let them leave the nest. With marriage denied to them, these daughters were kept as perpetual girls, their father's illness and their mother's need for company keeping them safely behind locked doors.

Princess Amelia was one such cosseted daughter, destined to spend her days under the watchful eye of her mother. From her birth in 1783 to her death in 1810, Amelia's life was short and beset by ill health, and yet she still found time to embark on the kind of doomed love affair best suited to the pages of romantic fiction.

Princess Amelia was the fifteenth and youngest child of George and Charlotte and she was born at the Royal Lodge, Windsor just three months after the sad death of 4–year-old Octavius, her father's favourite son. Octavius died just days after receiving the smallpox inoculation and the entire family was left understandably bereft, so the birth of Amelia was a bittersweet time at Windsor.

However the royal family doted on the little princess and gave her the diminutive nickname, 'Emily'. George, who was hit hardest of all by the death of Octavius, transferred his grieving adoration to his new daughter and soon she was the apple of his eye as her late brother had been before her, the king lavishing affection on this new addition to the household.

Amelia was just 5 years old when the king suffered his first episode of mental illness, leading the family down a path that would shatter their peaceful domestic life. As she grew older these periods of sickness grew more frequent and prolonged, until George's initial plans to take his youngest daughters to Hanover in search of husbands were eventually set aside. Despite his own happy marriage to Charlotte, George remained deeply unsettled by the miserable fate of his sister, Caroline Matilda, and had no desire to subject his girls to unfulfilled unions simply for politics and power. Even if he had, there could really be no question that he was well enough to make the journey, let alone properly broker marriage negotiations.

Since the king had no desperate wish to see his daughters married off, the princesses remained unbetrothed, neatly filling the need for companionship that so afflicted Queen Charlotte as her husband grew more disturbed. Into this secluded, secretive circle the girls were drawn, silent witnesses to their father's indisposition and their mother's unhappiness. No appropriate suitors existed at court and Amelia and her sisters were not exposed to society so, with little opportunity to meet gentlemen of their own, they settled into their quiet, domestic niche, watching as their happily married sister, the Princess Royal, flourished on the continent.

As a young lady, Amelia was plagued by ill health and when an infection in her knee left her badly debilitated, she was dispatched to Worthing to take the air and enjoy the benefits of sea bathing. Though she seemed to recover from that ailment, by 1798 she was already showing early signs of tuberculosis and her health took a turn for the worse once more.

This time, the sea cure prescribed for Amelia was to come from Weymouth and she travelled to the coast in the company of the Honourable Sir Charles FitzRoy, an equerry more than two decades her senior. During this fateful trip, Amelia and FitzRoy fell in love. They hoped that they might be allowed to marry but their dreams of domestic bliss were dashed when the queen refused to tell her husband of the affair. Terrified of the impact of such news on George's fragile mental health, Charlotte's decision meant the end of the couple's hopes for a happy ending as, without her family's consent, the princess could not hope to be married to her adored FitzRoy. She held out one final hope that the Privy Council might consent to the marriage but the young woman's failing health meant that she was never able to embark on this all-or-nothing plan.

The heartbroken young lady could not forgive her mother for standing in the way of her love and she must have felt the pain of unfulfilled longing keenly. However, she and FitzRoy continued to correspond and Amelia never lost hope that she might one day become the equerry's wife, even styling herself as *AFR*, Amelia FitzRoy.

Recalled to Windsor, Amelia grew increasingly despondent and in 1808 suffered a severe attack of measles, an infection that dramatically weakened her already frail body. In the summer of 1810 she took to her bed with Princess Mary as her constant companion and nurse, growing more unwell with every passing day. The intelligent, spirited young woman recognized that her life was drawing to an end and commissioned a mourning ring that would be given to the father who doted on her. She also took pains to ensure that she might make her farewells to the man she loved and, with the help of her sisters, FitzRoy was given leave to make visits to Amelia's bedside. One can only hope that the presence of her love gave Amelia some small comfort during her final, painful months yet it must also have reminded her of what she could not have and what her mother's refusal to pursue the marriage had cost her.

On 2 November 1810, as the family gathered to quietly celebrate Prince Edward's birthday, 27-year-old Princess Amelia passed away. Her final thoughts were for the man she loved and her dying words, related by Princess Mary in a letter to FitzRoy, were, 'Tell Charles I die blessing him.'[25]

The king was distraught at the loss of his youngest daughter and refused to accept that she was gone, the thought of losing another child was one that he simply could not bear. In his deluded state he concocted a belief that she was living in Hanover with a non-existent husband and brood of happy, healthy children, enjoying rude health and the best of everything. The royal family was plunged into deep mourning at her passing and it would be a long time before Amelia's siblings could begin to adjust to her loss. FitzRoy was not invited to attend the funeral at Windsor and bore his grief alone, comforted by the letters of Mary and her siblings.

The princess left her worldly possessions to Charles FitzRoy, the man to whom she had promised her hand in marriage. Her life cut tragically short, Princess Amelia was laid to rest in St George's Chapel at Windsor Castle, just three miles from the lodge where she had been born.

Dora and the Duke of Clarence

As comprehensively demonstrated elsewhere in this volume, the man who became George IV had something of a weakness for the ladies that began with his 'Perdita'. It was a trait shared by George's brother, William, Duke of Clarence, (later King William IV), and for him, a liaison with an actress was to result in a relationship that lasted for two decades and produced no less than ten children. With a track record like that one might hope for a happy ending but the lives of our Georgians were rarely predictable and however hard we might wish for a storybook finale, the truth was not so romantic.

Though she would enjoy huge fame under her stage moniker of Dorothea Jordan, when Dorothea Bland was born in Waterford, Ireland, in 1761, she did not appear destined for anything grand. Known to her family as Dora, she was one of five children of a stagehand who deserted his brood when Dora was just 13, plunging the family he left behind into poverty. Her mother, a jobbing actress, who had left her career behind to raise her children, decided to return to the stage. Of course, two workers in a family are better than one and with her she took young Dora, setting her on the first tentative steps of her celebrated career.

Once Dora hit the boards it became swiftly evident that she was born to perform and her prodigious acting talents were soon raising more than enough money to feed her family. She had a natural charm that eventually saw her become one of the most popular comic actresses of the era, particularly renowned for the breeches roles in which, dressed as a man, she was able to give the excitable audience a flash of her celebrated legs. However, professional triumph was followed by personal sadness and when Dora was all of 20, she embarked on an ill-advised affair with Richard Daly, the married manager of the Theatre Royal, Cork and a man to whom she already owed money. When Dora fell pregnant in 1782 she resolved to escape the controlling clutches of her lover and fled for a new start in England.

Here she joined Tate Wilkinson's theatre company and adopted the respectable new stage name of Mrs Jordan, inspired by the parallels between her braving the Irish Sea and the crossing of the River Jordan. Soon Dora's admirers had settled her debts to Daly, to whom she had borne a daughter, and in 1785 she joined the illustrious theatricals at Drury Lane.

As Dora's career flourished she embarked on a series of affairs, each more illustrious than the last. She took to her bed all manner of men, yet every time the romance ended in sadness for the actress, who never gave up her hopes of a happy ending. That dream seemed close to coming true when she embarked on a relationship with an ambitious lawyer and would-be politician, Richard Ford. In Ford, Dora was sure she had finally found the man who might offer the security that seemed to elude her, allowing herself to imagine life as his legitimate, respectable wife. Though she was by now one of the brightest stars on the London stage and revelling in her new found fame, Ford showed no inclination to celebrate Dora's professional success with an offer of marriage. He never told his lover that his intentions were not of the marrying kind and for years she persisted in her ambition until, with the birth of the couple's third child, Dora was forced to admit to herself that her dreams were destined never to come true. As she had done so many times, she packed up her belongings, said her sad goodbyes and moved on.

Where she moved on to, however, was quite another matter. This time there were no theatre managers or gentlemen of the legal profession; Dora already had someone waiting and he would outrank them all. True to her social climbing style, this latest beau just so happened to be William, Duke of Clarence, son of the king of Great Britain.

The Royal Marriages Act made a legal marriage between Dora and William most unlikely. With so many eligible Protestant princesses looking for a husband, the very idea of marriage to an Irish actress was unthinkable and had permission from the king or the Privy Council been sought and granted, the very history of Great Britain would have been changed forever. However, the Duke of Clarence wrongly assumed that he was unlikely to ever assume the throne and so had none of the attendant worries of producing an heir. This meant that he little cared whether his affair could be legitimized or not, so he and Dora simply ploughed their own romantic furrow.

The pair set up home together in Bushy House and lived together as man and wife, with the disapproving king powerless to intervene. The very happy couple made no secret of their relationship and over the years raised a family with what eventually grew to a brood of ten children, all of whom took the surname FitzClarence.

For twenty years the couple lived happily together; they may not have been married in the eyes of the law but they were certainly man and wife by any other name and when the end of the affair came, it was devastating. As the years passed it became apparent that the Prince Regent, with his disastrous marriage and tangled love life, was not going to produce a brace of heirs and even before his only legitimate child died, the pressure was on. The time had come for William to set aside the trifling matter of love and to concentrate on the serious business of finding a suitably respectable, noble bride who would play her part in ensuring the line of succession for the house of Hanover.

Suddenly faced with the very real possibility that he might one day sit on the throne, William knew that he could not do so with Dora by his side. One can only imagine the heartbreak Dora felt as she watched the man who she thought of as a husband bow and finally break under the pressure until, in 1811, he ended their relationship and began the search for a legitimate bride.

Heartbroken and humiliated, Dora pragmatically accepted a yearly payment worth over a quarter of a million pounds today. She was also awarded custody of the couple's daughters on the strict condition that she would not resume her acting career. However, when she was forced to break the condition three years later in order to raise enough money to pay off the debts of her son-in-law, William was as good as his word and took custody of the children who had remained with their mother.

It was the first of many catastrophic blows to Dora, the second coming when William slashed her allowance to reflect the fact that she no longer had the children to pay for. Dora had become used to living according to her rich means and showed no signs of tightening her stays, which meant that her debts inevitably began to climb. Soon she found herself unable to satisfy her many creditors and, fearing reprisals, fled for France. It was here that she died impoverished in 1816, the sad end to an adventurous life. Her descendants today include many noble names and even a twenty-first century prime minister – not bad for an illegitimate lass from Waterford.

A Delicate Scandal

The soubriquet 'Queen of Hearts' has become overused in recent years, bandied about by the press as though it is of the utmost profundity. In fact, it is an expression that might just as easily have been intended for Caroline of Brunswick, though of course, she was never crowned. One thing she was, much to her husband's chagrin, was the wronged wife, and the Prince of Wales did his very best to stir up scandals from which she could not escape, keen to make the point that, for all his womanizing, he was not always the party in the wrong.

George and Caroline's only child, Princess Charlotte of Wales, was born on 7 January 1796, almost nine months to the day from the couple's unhappy wedding night when the groom famously fell drunkenly to the floor of the marital chamber. This time there was to be no spare, and the couple parted company with a mutual relief matched only by the strength of their mutual animosity within a year of Charlotte's birth. Whilst the prince might have been glad to see the back of his far from adored wife, he had made a fatal miscalculation in the strength of her public following and for a man who was already far from popular, to leave the people of England with the belief that Caroline had been ill-used was unwise indeed. Subjected to the scrutiny and sharp tongue of Lady Jersey, George's mistress, and the utter contempt of her husband, she had endured all with dignity and good humour. Now, after bearing his child, she was cast out by that same husband as though she were nothing but a servant to be dismissed.

In 1797 the princess did exactly as her husband wished and granted him a separation, moving to her own residence. Here, free of George and Lady Jersey's watchful eye, Caroline decided to live a lot. Soon she was entertaining at every available opportunity and society gossips began to take notice of this once unassuming princess. A procession of men visited her home, they whispered with shocked delight, and barely a day passed by in which she wasn't engaged in some liaison or another. It was all too deliciously outrageous to be ignored.

In between setting the social scene alight and performing her charitable work, George did not believe that his wife had been idle in the bedroom and he was determined to prove it. After all, the future king of Great Britain could hardly be expected to live without the approbation of his subjects, but how could one fix a charge on a woman who was seemingly more sinned against saint than sinner?

Charlotte had a passion for adopting poor orphans and one of these, William Austin, joined her household as an infant in 1802. This was the touch paper that George needed and one of his many lady friends, Lady Douglas, was happy to light it. Although she had no grounds for the accusation, Lady Douglas made a claim that William was no orphan at all, but the son of Caroline and an unknown man and, worse still, that the princess had personally admitted as much to her.

The Prince of Wales seized upon the moment to play the wounded, wronged husband and demanded a full inquiry into this serious if baseless accusation. The 'Delicate Investigation', as it was known, was supposedly conducted in the utmost secrecy and began on 1 June 1806. It numbered amongst its participants some of the most illustrious names in British politics, with the Prime Minister, William Grenville, charged with determining whether Caroline had behaved as her husband and his friends claimed. Sitting alongside Grenville was the Lord Chancellor, Thomas Erskine, the Home Secretary, George Spencer and the Lord Chief Justice, Edward Law, Lord Ellenborough.

Before the inquiry, Lady Douglas repeated her allegation that Austin was Caroline's son and went on to elaborate even further. She told tales of scandal and sexual intrigues that engulfed any number of famous men, painting a picture of a house where debauchery was rampant and of a woman who never wanted for male company. When questioned on the veracity of her claims, the lady swore that every word was true. It is perhaps not coincidental that many of the names mentioned were senior Tory figures who championed the cause of Caroline as regent should the Prince of Wales die before he assumed the throne. Of course, it would be cynical in the extreme to suggest that Lady Douglas and George were motivated by politics and the need to keep Caroline from the centre of power at all costs, wouldn't it?

The commission charged with investigating the claims was convened by George III and gambled with the highest stakes imaginable, as noted in *The Morning Post* on 24 June 1806:

'The acts charged would, if proved, amount to no less than *high treason* in the illustrious personage: […] The nature of the accusation, amounting to what might eventually affect the succession of the crown; and the great stake the accusers put to hazard.'[26]

Of course, Caroline was not a saint but whether she had time to entertain quite the litany of lovers attributed to her bedchamber at Montague House is doubtful. At the request of Caroline, she was interviewed by lawyer and future prime minister (not to mention assassination victim), Spencer Perceval. Doctors were questioned on the matter of the pregnancy, domestic staff were quizzed regarding callers at the house yet the death blow to the rumours must surely have come when William's true parents, Sophia and Samuel Austin were summoned to give testimony. They told the commission that the little boy was indeed their child and had been given over to the care of Caroline in order to assure a better life for him, only enhancing her reputation as a lady of selfless philanthropy.

Whether this would come as any surprise to those following the case is certainly debatable. Reflecting the public mood, *The Morning Post* commented that the accusers were '*suspected* to be influenced by private pique'[27] and indeed, this is likely the case. As a confidante of both George and Caroline, it may be that Lady Douglas found her allegiances tested and chose the former. Perhaps Caroline *did* discuss indiscretions with her, but there was certainly little to question over the parentage of the young boy she had taken into her home.

With this damning evidence against the case of adultery and illegitimacy, the Delicate Investigation concluded six weeks after it had opened and declared that William was not Caroline's child, illegitimate or otherwise. However, it stopped short of exonerating her on charges of adultery and declared that she had not been proved innocent of that portion of the case. The victory was a slight one for George, who had hoped that William Austin was to prove his winning ticket. Instead, the consummate gambler had been left with a dud hand.

A later twist in the tale came when Caroline confessed to a friend that she *was* the child's mother, but she told another that she was caring for him on behalf of another European royal, who feared disgrace. Perhaps we should take these melodramatic claims with a pinch of salt, especially since William grew to strongly resemble other members of the Austin family, though he remained with Caroline until her death.

In the eyes of the public, the whole affair had not damaged Caroline one iota. As *Cobbett's Weekly Political Register* reflected indulgently on 18 October 1806, the only wrongs the princess had committed 'were a few trifling levities, such as every married woman in England was occasionally liable to'.[28] For a woman who had stood on charges of treason this was hardly the end of the world and both George and Caroline knew it. The prince had another card to play and in a show of monumental boorishness he made his next pawn the couple's own child, Princess Charlotte.

One unfortunate consequence of the investigation was that Caroline's access to Charlotte was restricted following the case, in keeping with George

III's decision that he should do something in response to the finding of likely adultery. Once Caroline's estranged husband became regent in 1811 these restrictions tightened still further until she barely saw her daughter at all and the distraught mother turned to politician Henry Brougham for help. A spin doctor before the term became fashionable, Brougham encouraged Caroline to fight back, painting her once again as the wronged wife yoked to a husband who did not care for her reputation nor the happiness of their child.

The Prince Regent struck back hard but as soon as the damning and supposedly confidential testimony that Lady Douglas had given during the Delicate Investigation seeped out, so too did the far more pro-Caroline statements of William Austin's mother. One thing that George seemed oblivious to was the impact of this war of attrition on his daughter, who caught between her parents, was instinctively minded to take her mother's side in matters scandalous. Seemingly blind to her distress, in 1814 George had the 18-year-old girl moved to an isolated new home at Cranbourne Lodge, Windsor, where she was virtually confined.

In an audacious bid for freedom, Charlotte literally ran from the house and fled for the safety of Caroline's home but it was to be a wasted effort. Her legal custodian was the Prince Regent and Brougham convinced the unhappy girl to return home. One hopes that Charlotte's desperate flight gave George pause for thought about his rash actions and following her return, father and daughter began a tentative reconciliation.

The young princess received a further blow later that same year when her mother confessed that she was to leave England and return home to Brunswick in return for a hefty payment from Parliament. It was a trip that Caroline, increasingly isolated and missing her homeland, had longed to make yet Charlotte was understandably distressed by the news, her access to her mother already severely limited as it was. In fact, Charlotte and Caroline would never meet again and just three years later, Princess Charlotte of Wales was dead.

Caroline finally left English shores on 8 August 1814, bound for Brunswick. After spending a fortnight in the company of her family she was on the road once more and there was no doubt that she was enjoying her new-found freedom. Her every move was reported to George by the agents employed to follow her but, free of the constraints of England, she went a little wild. Scandalously dressed and partying hard, Caroline gadded around the continent and eventually arrived in Italy, where a new scandal began to germinate.

In Milan, Caroline met former soldier, Bartolomeo Pergami and took him on as her chamberlain and, in all likelihood, a lot more besides. The pair became lovers in an entanglement that, had it happened in England, would have seen her tried for treason. She made no secret of the liaison and together the couple toured the Mediterranean, where Caroline appeared to be well and blissfully happy.

Of course, all of this was the source of no small annoyance to George who received reports of his wife's happy adventures with growing anger, his desire for a divorce increasing with each passing day. Funded by Parliament yet still spending more than she could afford, his estranged wife was making him look a fool in front of a populace that barely respected him. With only rumour to support the claims of adultery, the prince was powerless to take any action so when the chance came for a most cruel revenge, he seized it with both hands.

In November 1817, Princess Charlotte died as she gave birth to a stillborn son. As Charlotte's father and Caroline's husband, it fell to the Prince Regent to inform his wife that their only child was dead. The prince did no such thing and Caroline learned of her daughter's death in heartbreaking circumstances.

George wrote to the pope to inform him of the young woman's death and it was only by chance that the courier charged with delivering the message stopped in Pesaro, where Caroline had established her household. Quite by coincidence, he mentioned the unhappy message he was charged to convey and that is how Caroline learned of the death of her only child, third-hand, and entirely by accident. She was understandably heartbroken at the loss of her daughter and her estranged husband's callous disregard; no doubt it only strengthened her certainty that, in leaving George, she had made the right decision.

Tired of the ongoing humiliation of having a wife living it up in Italy with a strapping former soldier, in 1818, George convened the Milan Commission with the intention of proving his wife's adultery and gaining a divorce. With her relationship with Pergami an open secret, Caroline informed Brougham that she would consent to a divorce but would not, under any circumstances, admit adultery. She claimed to have remained faithful to her husband until they parted company, fidelity a value he could certainly not lay claim to. However, for the divorce to be allowed in England, one of the parties *had* to admit adultery and with neither willing to do so, the unhappy couple were left in deadlock.

Everything changed on 29 January 1820 with the death of George III. Suddenly Caroline was to all intents and purposes the queen, her husband the king. A king can hardly be seen to have a wife living openly with another man and with Caroline making plans to return to England and claim her place on the throne, Parliament panicked. They made a promise to Caroline that she would receive an annual payment of £50,000 (an increase of £15,000 on her current annuity) if she agreed to stay in Europe. Parliament prayed that Caroline would take money over prestige but her mind was made up: this was a matter of honour, and she was bound for England.

The English people rejoiced at the return of the queen on 5 June 1820 and when news of the celebrations reached George, it was a stinging blow. He responded by delivering the evidence of the Milan Commission to Parliament, determined now to prove that he should be given a divorce, that his saintly wife was far from innocent. On 27 June, Parliament began to examine the facts in the case and on 5 July, they made their verdict known with the introduction of the Pains and Penalties Bill.

The Bill was, to all intents and purposes, an attempt to place the queen on trial and would, if the charges were proven, see Caroline stripped of her title and the rank and privilege that went with it. Her marriage would be dissolved and she would, George hoped, be left in disgrace. Once again, the witnesses were called and the tale of Caroline's life on the continent became public knowledge. Far from scandal, treason and moral outrage though, the people rather liked the story of Caroline's settled household, where she and Pergami lived in quiet contentment. It was a marked and welcome contrast to what was happening in England, where George indulged in wildly public affairs, spent money as though it were going out of fashion and did little to honour the memory of his popular father. Radical forces rallied behind Caroline, seeing in her a figurehead for their fight against George and his supporters, leaving Parliament and court alike fearful that Britain stood on the brink of revolution.

The star witness for the prosecution was Theodore Majocchi, a servant from Caroline's household who was happy to testify to all manner of scandalous things to the Lords who questioned him. He told of shared beds, baths and carriages, of the couple spending time together in only their nightwear or underclothes and of many an intimate assignation. Like all of the prosecution witnesses, Majocchi found himself cast in the role of villain by the people of England, who saw little to admire in this apparent quisling. Jeered at and mocked, Majocchi was subjected to an unforgiving cross-examination by the formidable Brougham, who tore his scandalous statements to shreds.

In the end, the Bill never made the transition from Lords to Commons. With the voices of the people raised in support of Caroline it was simply abandoned despite passing the House of Lords. The public and press were united in their celebration of the collapse of the Bill, as mentioned in *The Morning Chronicle* of 11 November 1820 with the statement, 'We have at last satisfaction of congratulating the Country on the Abandonment of the Pains and Penalties Bill'.[29] Once again Caroline was the wounded party, her boorish husband the villain and, as the *Chronicle* stated, these 'odious proceedings'[30] had done fresh damage to his reputation in the country he ruled. Indeed, the passage of the Bill had 'done more to withdraw the affections of the people from the Constitutional authorities, than all the Revolutionary writings which ever were.'[31] As George licked his wounds, Caroline celebrated her victory to the resounding cheers of the English people, among whom 'the triumph of her MAJESTY is also [...] their triumph; for the successful resistance of oppression, the defeat of injustice, are causes for triumph truly worthy of a free and enlightened people a more general rejoicing was never known'.[32]

There was one final twist in the tale of Caroline of Brunswick and George IV. Seemingly untouchable, revelling in public popularity and riding high against her distrusted, widely-mocked husband, Caroline must have thought she was beyond reproach. Perhaps she had grown complacent, perhaps she was reckless or perhaps she simply underestimated the occasionally capricious nature of public opinion, but whatever her train of thought, it took just one dramatic final act to tarnish her glowing reputation.

The coronation of the king at Westminster Abbey on 19 July 1821 was a magnificent affair. George had waited a long time for this moment and intended that his would be the most memorable, flamboyant and expensive coronation that England had ever seen. With a party in the offing, the fickle public was whipped up into a pitch of patriotic fever, their dislike of George forgotten in their desire for the good knees up that the party-loving king was sure to give them. However, George knew that such a public event would be an ideal time for his estranged wife to make a nuisance of herself. He rightly guessed that Caroline might put in an appearance and took measures to ensure that his party would not be spoiled if she did. In and among the procession of herbstrewers, Officers of State, bishops, Barons of the Cinque Ports and peers of the realm were a number of suspiciously burly pages. These professional fighters were there to act as bodyguards and bouncers in the event that Caroline made a move.

George was right to be suspicious as Caroline did indeed show up to claim her place yet she was there and gone long before the procession started, arriving at Westminster Abbey as early as 6.00 am. Accompanied by Lord Hood and a gaggle of supporters, Caroline demanded entry to the abbey. Touring the various entrances to the building, she was finally assured that she could enter the Abbey only if she had a ticket, a humiliation to be sure. Lord Hood gallantly offered her his own ticket but, defeated, she returned to her carriage in embarrassment. As she retreated, one of the doorkeepers lost the battle to contain his laughter and the crowd, scenting blood, chimed in with laughter and jeers of their own.

For Caroline, this was a public relations disaster. Until this point, the people of England had been supportive of her well-publicized troubles with George, but with her appearance at the coronation the affection of the celebratory crowd evaporated. Caroline returned to Brandenburg House in humiliation and died within three weeks, finally giving her husband the freedom he had so long sought.

Although Caroline's death freed George from the marriage he hated, the manner of his release must have felt like a bittersweet victory. After all, he had devoted years of his life and untold angst to whipping up scandals to discredit his estranged wife, all to no avail. On each occasion she seemed to come out on top with the public and press, while George's behaviour and reputation suffered more and more. It is an irony, then, that Caroline's disastrous showing at Westminster Abbey was entirely of her own making. On this day George had created no conspiracy, called no witnesses and made no effort to discredit her. For one so aware of her place in the hearts of the English public, the reception she met must have come as a shock to the uncrowned queen and for the few weeks of her life that remained, she never overcame the humiliation.

Two Ladies of the Court

In our wander through royal marriages we peeked in on the domestic arrangements of Marie Joséphine of Savoy and Louis Stanislas, Count of Provence and future King of France. Married in 1771, the couple took an immediate dislike to one another and that far from ideal state of affairs was, depending on whose side you were on, thanks either to her dreadful personal hygiene and bad manners or his impotence and infidelity. Still, whatever lay behind the mutual discord, things could not go on and as the years passed, the ill-matched couple eventually drifted apart.

Of course, the noble houses of Europe were no strangers to unhappy marriages nor mistresses, affairs and domestic strife. Unlike our media-savvy twenty-first century world, even the most disastrous union could be presented to the public as a loving marriage but in the hothouse world of the royal court, there was nowhere to hide.

If mistresses to royal gentlemen were nothing to get het up over, the prospect of a mistress to a royal lady was a different prospect altogether. Although plenty of queens had good female friends and there was no shortage of rumours about Marie Antoinette and her inner circle, Marie Joséphine was about to discover that 'good friends' could sometimes be interpreted as something far more scandalous.

Unhappy in the gossip-driven court of Versailles, stuck with a husband who cared nothing for her and losing the popularity contest to her sister-in-law, Marie Antoinette, Marie Joséphine badly needed a friend. She found one in her lady-in-waiting, Marguerite de Gourbillon, and soon rumours began to spread that Marie Joséphine and Marguerite were far more than just chums. So close were the women that Louis Stanislas grew concerned at exactly what such an entanglement might do to *his* reputation as a husband, and with his pride at stake, he prevailed upon his brother, the king, to dismiss Marguerite.

No doubt Louis Stanislas breathed a sigh of relief when Marguerite was packed off to the coast in 1789, but that wasn't the end of this thorn in his side. The years passed and the Reign of Terror swept through France, claiming lives and beheading monarchs until, in 1795, Louis Stanislas was proclaimed king by the court in exile, though he was not recognized as such in his homeland for years to come.

By this time the couple was living separate lives and when Marie Joséphine returned to her homeland of Savoy, Marguerite reappeared in her life. Safely billeted in Russia with the exiled French court, the now rather grandly titled Louis XVIII no doubt ground his teeth at the news of his wife's reconciliation with her friend, his mood hardly improving once the two women set up home together in Schleswig-Holstein. However, Louis could not quite dismiss the nagging doubt that his public separation from his wife and her domestic arrangements would hardly do wonders for his status, let alone his royal authority… but what could he do to stop her?

The answer fell into the king's lap in 1799 thanks to a forthcoming royal wedding which provided Louis with the perfect excuse to summon his spouse to his side. With the court preparing to celebrate the nuptials of Marie Thérèse, the only surviving child of Louis XVI and Marie Antoinette, and her fiancé, Louis-Antoine, Duke of Angoulême, Louis put his foot down and ordered his wife to join him in Russia.

Just like today, Louis was mindful of the public relations value in presenting an apparently happy family to the world at what was to be a grand royal wedding. Accordingly, he informed his wife that her friend, Marguerite, was not invited to the ceremony. Not only that, she was not even invited to Russia and was expected to remain in Germany whilst Marie Joséphine carried out her queenly duty.

An outraged Marie Joséphine refused to even entertain the prospect of travelling without her friend and she and Marguerite set off together, no doubt adhering to the belief that Marguerite could hardly be turned away once she arrived in Russia. It was a dangerous gamble and one that didn't pay off as, before the women could arrive at the Jelgava Palace in Courland, they were stopped. Despite her royal friend's vehement protestations, Marguerite was ordered from the carriage and rather than cause a drama, she agreed to take separate accommodation whilst an outraged Marie Joséphine travelled on alone.

By the time she arrived at Jelgava Palace, Marie Joséphine was white with rage. She made a furious protest in front of the whole court, demanding that Marguerite be allowed to join her and refusing to change clothes or join the celebrations until she did. If she had hoped that such a public show of temper might do the trick she found her efforts frustrated and Louis flatly refused to allow his wife's companion into the palace. With little else to do but swallow her pride Marie Joséphine preferred instead to withdraw to her quarters and remained there, drinking herself into a stupor.

The very public display of Marie Joséphine's anger was the only gossip in town during the wedding and the court lapped up the scandal. This proved a pivotal moment for Marie Joséphine and Marguerite. Although they would continue to write to one another for years to come, the two women never lived alone together again and when Louis Stanislas left Russia to travel through Europe, Marie Joséphine went with him. Even now Marguerite followed them across the continent, finally settling in England once the royal couple took up residence at Hartwell House.

In fact, though they were ostensibly reunited, the king and queen's relationship did not really mellow until Marie Joséphine neared death in 1810. Confined to her bed, the queen took comfort in her husband's constant presence and before she died, their disagreements were set aside in one final act of reconciliation.

A Deadly Passion

In the 1700s, a scandal erupted in the royal palaces of Denmark that began in passion and ended in imprisonment, execution and upheaval. What started as a love affair between an unhappy young bride and an ambitious doctor spiralled into a political coup and even, some thought, the birth of an illegitimate child who was raised as a royal princess. It is far from a fairytale and the ending, when it came, was definitely not happily ever after.

The story began when Caroline Matilda of Great Britain, the youngest child of Frederick, Prince of Wales, and Princess Augusta of Saxe-Gotha, became betrothed to her cousin, King Christian VII of Denmark. The granddaughter of George II and sister of the future George III, Caroline Matilda's father died just a few months before her birth and she was raised in seclusion, a world away from the formal manners and customs of the Hanover court. She had little interest in royal life and enjoyed a simple existence, devoting herself to nature and equestrian pursuits. However, she was not exempt from the aristocratic marriage mart and soon the time had come to leave her rural idyll behind.

Caroline Matilda's quiet days ended at the age of 15 when the very reluctant princess travelled to Copenhagen to become the wife of her cousin, Christian VII of Denmark. Two years her senior and less than twelve months into his reign, Christian already enjoyed a reputation as something of an eccentric, though the full extent of his mental illness had yet to show itself. Once the severity of his condition became apparent, Caroline Matilda must have wondered what her life would become but for now, as she was joined in marriage to Christian at the Christiansborg Palace on 9 November 1766, she already found herself in a situation for which she was ill-prepared.

Reluctant to consummate the marriage, Christian preferred to spend his time with courtesans and prostitutes, enthusiastically frequenting the brothels of the city whilst rejecting all contact with his wife. As Christian began to exhibit ever more bizarre behaviour, the only thing that mattered to his advisers was that the royal couple must provide an heir, regardless of what husband and wife might think of one another. The spare could wait, but with a king who appeared to be mad, having neither heir nor regent ready to take the reins was a recipe for disaster. The reluctant Christian eventually capitulated and the no doubt very romantic consummation of the marriage took place. Caroline Matilda's pregnancy was announced, and the court heaved a collective sigh of relief when on 28 January 1768, the queen gave birth to a healthy son, the future Frederick VI.

Her duty fulfilled, Caroline Matilda was once again set aside by her husband. One can only imagine that this must have been quite a relief because by this point, even the most loyal courtier could not help but notice that the king was far from stable. Christian's paranoia deepened to a frightening extent and when he took the decision to bring doctor Johann Friedrich Struensee to Denmark, the relief at court was palpable. Finally it seemed that the troubled monarch had recognized his declining mental health and taken decisive action, choosing the stabilizing doctor to care for him. Struensee was welcomed with open arms by courtiers and for once, all seemed calm in Denmark.

It would not last.

The Prussian Struensee trained as a doctor at the University of Halle and his intelligence and charm gained him entry to the grandest circles in society. Through his involvement in Enlightenment theory he came to know the Danish aristocrat, Count Schack Carl Rantzau, and when Christian decided to undertake a tour of Europe, Rantzau was quick to recommend Struensee as the ideal physician to accompany the king.

Struensee and Christian spent months together and became firm friends, with the king soon coming to trust him above any other. Upon their return to Denmark in 1769 the doctor was awarded a position as State Councillor and was soon winning friends at the Oldenburg court. It was particularly ironic given what came later that Caroline Matilda was not among his admirers at the start, whereas those who *had* championed him turned against the doctor as the months went on.

Isolated and ignored by her husband, the queen was unsure of the influence the physician wielded over the king, yet in time she set these doubts aside as he became first her friend and then her lover. Although he seemed able to quell the worst of the king's eccentricities, Struensee's interests soon extended far beyond the medical care of the monarch and as Christian descended deeper into madness, so Struensee's influence at court increased. In 1770, he was elected privy counsellor and with the monarch by now all but insensible, his former doctor enjoyed a period of virtually unchallenged authority. On top of that, he won Caroline Matilda's trust and affection when his intervention saved the life of her son during an agonizing battle with smallpox. The lonely queen and ambitious physician soon fell in love and embarked on a passionate, heated affair.

The relationship between doctor and queen was an open secret and it is unlikely that the king did not know of it. One might have expected Christian to be disturbed by these developments but he delighted in the unusual arrangement, glad to see his wife happy, his own marital responsibilities discharged, and the burden of government business lifted from his sagging shoulders.

A virtual regent, Struensee initiated over a thousand reforms that began with the total restructure of the unwieldy Danish cabinet and reached far and wide. At first the public warmed to Struensee yet the rush of new laws soon began to try their patience as they witnessed what they were sure was a hunger for power running out of control. With the guidance and support of the queen, Struensee's reforms included the abolition of torture, the banning of slavery and widespread vaccination against smallpox for the poorest children in Denmark. Of course, his experimental inoculation against the disease had been what first brought him to Caroline Matilda's attention when his decisive actions saved the life of her son.

The 'Time of the Struensee' was over within sixteen months. Outraged by Caroline Matilda's open liaisons with the doctor and her proclivities for dressing as a man and mixing with the populace of Copenhagen, the ruling classes decided that something simply must be done about this unruly pair. Facing higher taxes, reduced privilege and more reforms than they knew what to do with, the cabinet and court turned against the queen and her lover, their previously anaemic support for Christian returning with fervour. Struensee compounded the situation by enacting a wholesale dismissal of officials and installing members of his own circle in positions of authority. Tired of watching her stepson being sidelined and hungry for some influence of her own, Queen Dowager Juliana Maria encouraged the once pro-Struensee Count Rantzau to take action against the meddling doctor once and for all.

When the queen gave birth to a daughter, who was widely assumed to be Struensee's child, his opponents moved in earnest against him. On 17 January 1772, Caroline Matilda and Struensee were arrested at Christiansborg Palace. The former royal physician was charged with usurping royal authority and was subjected to interrogation and torture. As the king toured Copenhagen waving happily to the joyous crowds who gathered to see him, his queen was spirited away to Kronborg Castle and held as a prisoner. It was here that she heard that her marriage had been dissolved, which was a blow if not a surprise.

For Struensee, however, things were to end more brutally. He mounted an eloquent and passionate defence of his actions but the die was already cast and the reformer was sentenced to have his hand severed and then to be beheaded, drawn and quartered. He was held in readiness for execution at Kastellet in Copenhagen and on 28 April 1772 went to his death before a crowd of thousands who had gathered to witness the downfall of this once powerful man.

Though her son remained in Copenhagen with his father, Caroline Matilda and her daughter were kept in isolation at Kronborg Castle. Of course, there is little point in having a king for a brother if you don't make use of the resource and George III successfully petitioned to have his sister and niece released from prison and sent into exile in the Hanoverian Celle Castle. He stopped short of asking for her to be returned to England, however, perhaps mindful of the scandal that her name evoked. Her unhappy fate forever coloured George III's opinion of arranged marriages and when his own girls were old enough to find husbands, the memory of Caroline Matilda left him fearful of subjecting them to a life of dutiful misery.

Here in Celle, where George I's own wife had been born, the disgraced former queen devoted herself to philanthropy, but she did not lose her love for politics. In the few years that remained of her life she planned for the far off day when she might depose Christian and rule as regent until her son reached the age of majority. In fact, Caroline Matilda never saw Denmark nor her son again and she died of scarlet fever at the age of just 23. With no mother to care for her, the queen's daughter, Princess Louise Auguste of Denmark was returned to court and a life of popularity and privilege but for Caroline Matilda, there was to be a final, tragic coda.

Despite his intervention in her imprisonment, even in death George III rejected calls for Caroline Matilda to be returned to England. She had wished to be interred in Westminster Abbey but this final request was denied. Instead, the late queen was laid to rest in her place of exile at Celle, the final stop in a life that had been short, scandalous and ultimately tragic

Act Four

Death

'That we must all die, we always knew; I wish I had remembered it sooner.'

Samuel Johnson, 1784

From the glittering hallways of Versailles to the lonely seclusion of Celle Castle, even the divine right of kings must one day yield to a greater authority. Whether an iron-fisted absolutist or a government-shackled figurehead, the Georgian monarchs were no better placed than paupers or merchants to escape the inevitable spectre of death and when he came calling on the crowned heads of the Georgian era, it was often in flamboyant, grisly style.

In an era when medicine was a hit and miss affair and royal physicians wielded enormous power at court, it is perhaps of little surprise that not all members of the royal houses died peacefully in their beds. This is not a collection of tales for the faint of heart, nor for those who fear the leech and a little bloodletting, let alone the cold steel of the court doctor's knives. If the very mention of gangrene sends a chill through your marrow, look away now.

Prepare to mount the scaffold and hear the thud of the National Razor; witness the writhing agony of the king who sat on the throne at the Bourbon Restoration and heed the lesson of King George IV, so loathed that *The Times* mocked his passing even as he went to his grave. In the pages that follow, childbirth ends in a surgical nightmare, a mighty empress suddenly turns purple and a cricketing prince meets a fitting end. Let us now creep along the hallways of the castles and palaces of Europe and take a respectful peek at the final hours of the Georgian royals.

'A Weary Traveller': The Birth of Georgian Britain

Anne, Queen of Great Britain (Stuart)

London, England, 6 February 1665–

London, England, 1 August 1714

Before you question the inclusion of Queen Anne, the last Stuart monarch of Britain, in a work on the Georgian era, pray let me take a moment to explain. When Anne died in her forties, she left no heir to take her place on the throne and, with seventeen pregnancies, it was not for the want of trying. All but five of those pregnancies ended in miscarriage or stillbirth and of those children who were delivered into the world, only one lived past infancy. That lucky child was Prince William, Duke of Gloucester, sole heir to the Stuart throne of England. The court celebrated, while the queen and her husband, Prince George of Denmark, breathed a sigh of relief and for a while at least, all seemed well.

Of course, fate had other plans for the house of Stuart and far away on the continent, Anne's second cousin, George, Elector of Hanover, was about to find himself thrust into one of the brightest royal spotlights in Europe. Never particularly robust, by the age of 10, the Duke of Gloucester was not well at all and suddenly the concept of an heir and a spare seemed horribly prescient in the Stuart household. The little duke died in 1700, just a week after his eleventh birthday, plunging the English monarchy into a succession crisis. Anne was the heir and the cause of Protestantism in England looked to her as all that stood between the throne of England and a Catholic restoration yet, with a miscarriage as recent as January that same year, it seemed there was no question that Anne would be able to provide another heir to take up the reins.

It was at this point that Parliament took action to focus their considerable resources on preventing the dreaded Catholic restoration. Their response to the crisis was to legislate and in 1701, the Act of Settlement was passed. The Act ruled that, should Anne or the current incumbent, her brother-in-law, William III, fail to provide an heir, then the crown would pass to Sophia, Electress of Hanover; should Sophia predecease Anne, then the English crown would pass to her nearest descendent. The Act also contained the vital clause that no Catholic could sit on the throne, and should the heir or Sovereign marry a Catholic then they would be removed from the line of succession.

Well aware that her reign would be the last of the Stuart line, Anne inherited the throne of England, Scotland and Ireland upon the death of William III in 1702. Already crippled by years of gout, the new queen did not fall pregnant again and instead concentrated on fulfilling the duties of her role, presiding over the War of Spanish Succession and taking an active interest in political decisions, whilst never appearing to be anything other than utterly delighted about the now inevitable Hanoverian succession.

Regardless of her feelings on the matter, by the summer of 1713, it was obvious to everyone who knew the queen that the Hanoverians would soon be taking up residence in England. Anne had endured a year or more of ill health, confined to her bed by a fever so severe that the court and country began to whisper that death would soon be upon her. Well used to battling with such drama, Anne recovered her health by Christmas yet she was frailer than she had ever been and found herself immediately drawn into a mentally exhausting political intrigue orchestrated by Robert Harley, Lord Treasurer.

Perhaps sensing that death was near, Anne was determined not to be undermined at such a pivotal moment in her life. Dangerously ill and growing weaker by the day, the queen dismissed Harley and continued to attend Cabinet meetings despite her sickly condition. Barely able to lift her head, she endured debate sessions that lasted from dusk to dawn, searching for an appropriate and loyal successor to the deposed Harley. It was a decision that Anne was destined never to make.

On 30 July, the day on which the final Cabinet meeting was due to be held, the queen suffered a stroke so severe that it robbed her of the power of speech. This time there would be no recovery and she lingered for no more than a day, finally taking her last breath at 7.30 am on 1 August 1714. Anne was buried alongside her husband and the children who had predeceased her and, as the Stuart monarchs passed into history, the Georgian era dawned.

The Sunset of the Sun King

Louis XIV, King of France and Navarre (Bourbon)

Saint-Germain-en-Laye, France, 5 September 1638–

Versailles, France, 1 September 1715

In royal history the name of Louis XIV, or the Sun King, is almost legendary. His reign of seventy-two years remains the longest of any European monarch and he left behind a legacy of absolutism that endured for generations, ended only by the keen blades of the French Revolution. Though Louis XIV died decades before the clouds of discontent gathered over the country, when the sun set on the Sun King, it was painful, grisly and far from regal.

Since the days of his youth, Louis XIV had been a keen outdoorsman; he loved to shake off the cares of office with a day of sport and hunting was one of his favourite pastimes. Even in his seventies Louis adored the thrill of the chase and on the fine summer morning of 10 August 1715, he decided that there could be no better way to make the best of the weather than to spend the day hunting at his royal residence in Marly. As Louis enjoyed these carefree hours his pleasure was marred somewhat by a sharp pain that stabbed at his leg. Suspecting an injury, the agonized monarch cut short the hunt and requested that his doctor, Guy-Crescent Fagon, be summoned. The physician examined his illustrious patient and, weighing up the symptoms, made a confident diagnosis of sciatica.

Confident, but wrong.

As the days passed and the agony did not ease, an alarmed Louis noticed black marks appearing on his leg, a sure sign of gangrene. Even then the learned Fagon steadfastly stuck to his initial diagnosis of sciatica with a self-assurance borne out of years of professional authority. As so many of his contemporaries would do when suffering from appalling ailments that would lay even the most robust person low, the king attempted to continue with business as usual. However, the pain grew steadily worse until he was forced to retire to his bed at Versailles. Even if Fagon had immediately treated the gangrene, it was too late to save Louis and the king would not leave his chamber alive again.

The Sun King endured a final week of unimaginable torment, gangrene making its fatal, unstoppable way through his body. Sure that he was nearing the end, Louis began to put in place plans for his succession, determined to leave every thread neatly tied when his last moments came. With farewells made to courtiers and friends, Louis sank into a delirium and just after 8.00 am on the morning of 1 September 1715, the Sun King died.

Having lain in state for a week, the remains of the king were transferred to the Saint-Denis Basilica, where they would remain until they were exhumed during the French Revolution. Perhaps in the future his monumental reign will be exceeded but in the history of the European monarchy, the Sun King will remain iconic... his doctor less so.

Death on the Road

George I, King of Great Britain and Ireland (Hanover)
Osnabrück, Hanover, 28 May 1660–Osnabrück, Hanover, 11 June 1727

In George I's eventful life, one thing in particular held true: from birth to death, he loved his birthplace of Hanover and but for the obligations forced on him by the Act of Settlement, he would never have left it. With this in mind, it seems fitting, then, that George did not die on English soil or anywhere near it; instead, the first Hanoverian king of Great Britain took his last breath during a visit to his beloved native land.

Since his coronation in 1714, the country of George's birth was never far from his mind. Although he had little choice but to take up permanent residence in England, his restlessness was evident from the many trips he took back to the land where he had spent his formative years. Long periods passed in which the king immersed himself once more in Hanoverian life, happy to let England rub along without him. The last of these nostalgic journeys came in 1727 and was, as ever, undertaken in the company of his long-term mistress, Melusine von der Schulenberg, Duchess of Kendal.

It was, on reflection, perhaps not wise of a man nearing 70 to submit himself to the arduous travel that such a trip involved, but one cannot easily tell a king where he might go and so the entourage set off to the land of George's birth. The elderly king's health took a turn for the worst on 9 June 1727 when, as the group travelled between Delden and Nordhorn, he suffered a major stroke. Barely clinging to life, the monarch was rushed to the comfort of Schloss Osnabrück, home of his brother, Ernest Augustus, Duke of York and Albany. In the land where he had been born, the king lingered on the verge of death for two days. He finally passed away in the early hours of 11 June, ending the reign of the first monarch of the Georgian era. Melusine couldn't quite accept the loss, and following the death of the man she adored, she devoted herself to the care of a pet raven that she believed was the spirit of the king returned to her side.

Whether his spirit inhabited Melusine's avian companion is debatable but whilst she whispered sweet nothings to her raven, George I was laid to rest in the chapel of the Leineschloss. Centuries later he took one final trip, when the palace was destroyed by bombing raids during World War II, George was removed and reburied at Herrenhausen, where he remains to this day.

'Harness my sledge'

Peter II, Emperor and Autocrat of all the Russias (Romanov)
St Petersburg, Russia, 23 October 1715–Moscow, Russia, 30 January 1730

There are some twists that even fiction writers shy away from as that little bit *too* mawkish, straining credibility perhaps further than they might want and, surely, killing someone off on their wedding day is one of those. Add to that the fact that the deceased groom was all of 14 years of age and the stage seems set for a story that is too grim to be true.

Emperor Peter II of Russia was a young man who packed much into his short life. The son of the late Tsarevich Alexei and Princess Charlotte Christine of Brunswick-Lüneburg, Peter's royal pedigree was cemented by the small matter that his grandfather was none other than Peter the Great. The young man had ruled Russia since the age of 12 yet it was not a responsibility he particularly relished, his childhood consumed by the duties of state with barely a moment for him to gather himself for the challenges that might one day lay ahead.

To make matters worse, Peter was not looking forward to his imminent wedding to Ekaterina Dolgorukova and the 18-year-old bride wasn't particularly thrilled about the proposed match either. However, an emperor needs an empress and with all arrangements set in place, the wedding was scheduled for January 1730. It is, of course, strange for a modern royal-watcher to imagine these marriages commissioned and carried out in childhood but such was the lot of the eighteenth century power brokers.

As 1729 drew to a freezing close, Peter was already in poor health, suffering from a severe and debilitating cold. He had been well-schooled in his responsibilities though and, with his sense of duty outweighing all else, continued to honour his formal engagements. So as the New Year dawned with a traditional Epiphany Day feast on the bitterly cold banks of the River Moscow, Peter was in attendance, shivering in the plummeting temperatures. It was during this engagement that the young man's fragile condition deteriorated and as he slipped into a delirium, he was rushed back to Lefortovo Palace to be assessed by the royal physicians.

And we all know what good that did some of his contemporaries…

After an examination the doctors gravely declared that the teenage ruler was infected with the dreaded, often deadly smallpox and that time was short, with no hope of recovery. Barely coherent, Peter expressed a wish to see his late sister, who had died two years earlier and feverishly called for his sledge. Just minutes later as dawn broke over Moscow, Peter II died and with him, the direct male line of the Romanov dynasty reached its end.

A Historic Hernia

Caroline of Ansbach, Queen of Great Britain and Ireland (Hanover)
Ansbach, Holy Roman Empire, 11 March 1683–London, England,
1 December 1737

If Caroline of Ansbach, wife of George II, had departed this life peacefully in her sleep then she would not be afforded a place here among these gruesome or otherwise noteworthy deaths. However, Caroline's final days were anything but pleasant, involving a surgical catastrophe, rivers of bodily fluids and the sort of stench that would wilt flowers.

This is not a story for the faint of heart or those of a squeamish disposition so now you have been duly warned, let us embark on the tale…

Since her husband's coronation a decade earlier, the personable Caroline had won many admirers in her adopted country, proving herself to be an able and fair regent during his absences. She provided an heir and a spare and even championed the practice of variolation in the ongoing Georgian battle against smallpox, not to mention putting up with the vagaries of her famously capricious husband. Of course, she was considerably less popular with her own son, Frederick, Prince of Wales, than with the people of England, but one can't have everything.

Determined to do her duty to her husband and ensure the succession of his line, Caroline became pregnant no fewer than ten times. Although eight of the babies were born alive, the repeated pregnancies took an enormous toll on Caroline's health. Indeed, it was an untreated umbilical hernia suffered earlier in life that came back to haunt her in grisly style years later.

Whilst pregnancy and labour were necessary risks for any royal wife, gout was virtually an occupational hazard among Georgian aristocracy and Caroline was just one of many who suffered from the agonizing ailment. She maintained her mobility to some extent but weight gain left her fond of a wheelchair in which, during attacks, she would whizz around her home conducting her affairs. Still, Caroline took her ailments in her hobbled stride, until, in early November 1737, she was struck down by a violent pain that tore through her abdomen.

Despite the fact that she was so wracked by agony that she could barely stand, even then the queen tried not to create a fuss. It was with some reluctance that she agreed to retire to her rooms at St James's Palace and await the royal physicians, led by John Ranby. The learned doctors eventually decided that Caroline's womb had ruptured and, with time of the essence, they set about bleeding their patient. Once it became apparent that this was going to achieve nothing, the doctors attempted a surgical intervention and the unfathomably stoic queen endured these unanesthetized procedures without complaint, though she grew weaker with every passing day.

There was, however, one extremely pertinent bit of information that Caroline and George had chosen not to share, and that was the matter of the hernia she had suffered during her last pregnancy in 1724. Why Caroline chose to conceal the condition must remain a mystery; perhaps she felt it marked her as a failure or somehow less of a woman, perhaps she simply hoped that it might just go away but the neglected condition grew more and more serious. Only when the varied and debilitating treatments ended in failure did Caroline face the stark reality that she must tell the truth and submit to whatever procedure her doctors deemed necessary. Finally, with no other choice available to her, the queen told Ranby of the hernia she had suffered more than a decade earlier.

As soon as he learned of the concealed condition, the doctor set to work. Upon further investigations it became all too obvious that the long-ignored hernia had taken an aggressive hold of the queen, causing part of her bowel to decay. In the gruesome procedure that followed, the physicians made the unimaginable decision to actually slice out the decayed flesh they found around the hernia, apparently not recognizing the inevitable outcome of such a procedure. The operation had the effect of completely opening Caroline's bowels and caused catastrophic, irreversible internal injury. From that day forward the fate of Caroline of Ansbach was sealed as her bowels were opened by the very doctors who were entrusted to save her. She suffered violent fits of vomiting and raw excrement oozed into her abdomen, horrifically seeping out through the surgical wounds. Despite her terrible suffering Caroline clung weakly to life, enduring untold agony with every moment.

The palace air grew thick and heavy with the sickening stench of excrement and decay that filled the queen's chambers for the last week of her life as with each passing day she grew weaker. George was her constant and devoted companion in these final days, never leaving his wife's side as she drew closer to her grave. Never the most faithful spouse, George was seemingly transformed by the sight of his suffering wife and though she implored him to remarry once she was gone, he refused to even countenance the idea. Instead, he said, he would take mistresses, as no woman could match her as his bride. This may not seem like a particularly romantic sentiment but royal mistresses were a fact of life that Caroline had long been resigned to; for George to swear never to remarry though… well, that was a sign of true devotion.

Attended to and prayed for by her husband and daughter, Amelia, Charlotte's dreadful suffering finally reached what must have seemed like a merciful end at 10.00 pm on a winter night in 1737 when she reached out for the king's hand and told him with her final, agonized breath, 'I am going.'

The queen died at that moment, finally released from the agonies of her final days. Her death plunged public, court and her own family into deep mourning and George kept his promise, never taking another woman as his bride. Caroline of Ansbach was buried in Westminster Abbey and when her husband joined her in death, their coffins were placed together and the sides removed, so that they might rest together for all eternity.

The Death of a Westphalian Ham

Anna, Empress and Autocrat of All the Russias (Romanov)

Moscow, Russia, 7 February 1693–
St Petersburg, Russia, 28 October 1740

Throughout the history of Europe, there have been all kinds of rulers. Some are gentle and benevolent, some political, some passionate whilst others are not that interested in the ruling side of things at all, preferring to spend their days in more leisurely pursuits. For now though, we are concerned with another type of ruler, those who take the business of being Sovereign very seriously indeed.

Empress Anna of Russia, memorably described by Thomas Carlyle as possessing 'such a *cheek* the Pictures give her, in size and somewhat in expression like a Westphalia ham',[33] was one such ruler. Autocratic, strong-minded and with an understanding of court, politics and strategy that could certainly shame many of her contemporaries, Anna was not a lady who took any form of weakness lightly, including her own. She was so determined that when her own twilight began to loom, she dealt with the matter just as she would any other business and took the grim reaper firmly by the scythe!

The Empress and Autocrat of all the Russias had spent a decade of ironclad rule at the helm of her country, and yet as the years passed by it became worryingly apparent to both Anna and all who knew her that her health was not what it had once been. True to political form she did not make her first priority her own medical care, but instead focused on the matter of who would occupy the throne once she inevitably departed it.

Nothing was more important to the ailing empress than ensuring that her influence continued after her death. A widow for some thirty years,

Anna had no children to inherit the throne. Instead she favoured her long-time favourite, Ernst Johann von Biron, Duke of Courland and Semigallia, and he certainly had no complaints. Still, the power-loving empress seemed reluctant to sign the final papers confirming his appointment and procrastinated again and again, the dotted line remaining firmly devoid of her signature. The constant and unsubtle lobbying by Biron for Anna to seal his fate in power raised a few eyebrows among those who thought that he was no stranger to her bedchamber, though of course, this gossip was kept firmly away from the fearsome lady herself.

Plagued by concerns for the succession, Anna tried not to surrender to the many and varied ailments that plagued her. For years she had been nearly crippled by gout and left so long untreated, the illness took up aggressive residence and left the empress virtually immobile. Perhaps the not inconsiderable agony of her gout initially distracted Anna from the unexplained pains that began to wrack her torso; the first signs of the kidney problems that would kill her, but eventually the day came when they were too severe to ignore.

As 1740 wore on, Anna's agony grew worse until her doctors diagnosed an ulcer on one kidney. Rather than worry their patient, the physicians took the somewhat patronizing decision to tell the dying woman that she was suffering from nothing more than the menopause. Of course, it was an unsuccessful ploy and she was perfectly well aware that such agony could only be the result of something serious. Soon Anna began to experience other symptoms, the ulcers giving way to kidney stones that no amount of bleeding or salves could treat.

When Anna experienced a seizure in October 1740 that left her bedbound, it became apparent to all that a decision on the succession had to be made as a matter of utmost urgency and once again, Biron renewed his efforts. He hoped to serve as ruler until Anna's infant grandnephew, Ivan VI was old enough to take his rightful place as Emperor and Autocrat of All the Russias but he could not do this alone. No matter whether the regent-to-be had achieved his role through more physical favours, the lady's word was law and she *had* to name him before her death, or he would never achieve his ambitions.

There was no question that Anna favoured the doomed Ivan as her successor but the boy was still a babe in arms and his mother, Anna, was as keen as Biron to take the throne as regent. As the empress lay dying, Biron was a constant presence at her side, clutching the unsigned will that would guarantee him the throne and encouraging her to sign her name to the document. Finally, in the closing days of her life, Anna took up her pen, signed her name and gave Biron what he wanted. With that signature, the responsibility for ruling Russia finally fell into his outstretched hands.

Anna died of kidney failure at just 47, her absolutist reign at an end. In a final twist of fate, Biron's hard-fought battle for the throne of Russia fell apart almost immediately. Before Anna had even been laid to rest in the Peter and Paul Cathedral, the succession of Russia had descended into turmoil.

The Fungi that Felled an Emperor

Charles VI, Holy Roman Emperor (Habsburg)

Vienna, Austria, 1 October 1685–

Vienna, Austria, 20 October 1740

This is the story of how a fatal fungi and how a pot of stewed mushrooms led to war.

There was nothing my grandfather liked more than a ramble in Sherwood Forest and my memory of happy summer outings with him are innumerable and cherished. There was little he didn't know about the countryside and one piece of his advice always stuck with me: wild mushrooms are best left alone.

Charles VI, Holy Roman Emperor, might have done well to heed that bit of advice or at the very least to make sure that his cook was educated on the types of flora and their various toxins. Sadly this particular element of culinary training appears to have been overlooked and it was to have painful, fatal consequences for the head of the house of Habsburg.

In October 1740, it was fair to say that Charles VI was at a low ebb. Beset by political intrigue, tormented by territorial disputes and facing possible financial ruin, fate decided that what the emperor needed was a catastrophic punchline to his already trying year. Charles, on the other hand, wanted only a simple pleasure, a little respite from his stress, and off he went in search of an indulgent bowl or two of comfort food.

Charles already had something of a sniffle and with the worries of the world piling on his shoulders, the monarch decided to take the advice of the old wives' tale to feed a cold, starve a fever. He set out to assuage his hunger and found solace in his favourite dish, a meal of mushrooms stewed in Catalan oil. He dined royally on that fateful evening, taking plateful after plateful of the nourishing stew and all the time he was hastening towards a most terrible end. Those seemingly innocent mushrooms were anything but and, quite by accident, the Holy Roman Emperor had filled his belly with highly toxic death cap mushrooms.

Within hours of wolfing down his dinner, Charles was writhing in the grip of a terrible digestive disorder. The court physicians were summoned yet found themselves utterly at a loss for a diagnosis and with no clue as to the cause of the problem; there was little they could offer in the way of treatment. For ten long and painful days the unfortunate emperor lingered on in agony as his physicians argued amongst themselves, every treatment at their disposal doing nothing to lessen their monarch's suffering. At a loss as to what else to do, his advisers decided to move Charles to the Favorita Palace in Vienna, where they hoped that a change of air might prove beneficial.

Of course, a change of air is of little use when it comes to highly toxic mushroom stew and on 20 October 1740, Charles VI died. That simple plate of mushrooms and Catalan oil had wreaked a terrible havoc and set in motion a succession crisis that would engulf the late emperor's lands and house for almost a decade.

A Fatal Wicket

Frederick Louis, Prince of Wales (Hanover)

Hanover, Germany, 1 February 1707–
London, England, 31 March 1751

There is a belief that when your time comes to depart this world, it is better to die doing something you love. Of the gardeners who fall down dead in their rose gardens, the cooks found slumped over their dough and the rambler who sits down for a rest and never stands up, it is said time and again: 'At least they died doing something they loved'. Legend has it that Frederick, Prince of Wales, did not exactly die in the commission of his hobby but was, in a roundabout way killed by it.

Well, why let the facts get in the way of a poignant story?

Elsewhere in these pages we have read of Frederick's early life; of his separation from his parents, his frankly hostile relationship with them when finally reunited and his determination to live his life according to his own wishes, not those of his kingly father, George II. The struggle to be true to himself in the face of family expectation was one that Frederick would never reconcile and it began long before he arrived in England, yet it was here that it became more challenging than ever.

When the Prince of Wales arrived in England in 1728, he took one look at this new land and decided that it would suit him very well indeed. He delighted in the society of his new home, and did all he could to establish an active social life, eventually, taking an interest in the most English game of cricket.

With his new friends, Frederick threw himself into the sport with gusto. He became absolutely passionate about the game, both as a spectator and gambler, making wagers and cheering on the players alongside his fellow enthusiasts. The Prince of Wales did nothing by halves and soon he was considered something of an expert on his adopted sport, often to be seen watching matches and socializing with both players and fans of the game.

As is so often the way with a hobby held dear, Frederick wasn't content to just watch and he wanted to do more than simply stand on the side of the pitch. Instead he strode out to the wicket, bat in hand and honed his skills.

Soon even *this* wasn't enough for the young prince who liked to be at the heart of the action and in September 1731 he took up the bat on Kennington Common to compete in his first professional match. Sadly, we cannot know whether Frederick set the pitch on fire as no record survives of his performance, but his participation was sufficiently novel to be reported in advertisements for the match. His appearances at other games were well-documented by the popular press and soon cricket and Frederick were inseparably linked.

Often on hand to present prizes to winning teams, Frederick also awarded his favourite players from his own pocket, playing in and captaining matches whenever the opportunity arose. The prince's passion for cricket never dimmed and he played and spectated with the same enthusiasm and commitment to the game that he had shown from the start. Perhaps this was a way for Frederick to escape the problems of home, the expectations of family and the conflicts with his parents. Here on the cricket pitch he was one of a team, surrounded by those who shared his love for a simple matter of sport.

Of course, there *has* to be a dark twist to the prince's love of the game, or he wouldn't be here in our gad about the deathbeds of the Georgian royals!

Frederick fell ill with a serious cold in the early months of 1751 and took to his bed under the care of his physicians. Augusta, his heavily pregnant wife, kept a watchful eye on her husband and even the king, with whom his relationship was so fraught, sent for word regarding the health of his son. Although the prince's condition did not seem to deteriorate as the weeks passed, nor did it seem to improve and when the end came, it was swift and unstoppable.

As had become his custom, Frederick received his doctors and family into his room and for a time all seemed relatively peaceful. However, as the physicians were preparing to leave, Frederick began to choke. On and on went the choking until he ceased abruptly and told those around him, 'Je sens la mort'.[34] With those final words, 44-year-old Frederick died, the victim of a burst abscess in his lung.

Soon word began to spread that days earlier, the prince had been struck in the chest by a cricket ball and this had caused the abscess to burst. Ironic and tragic though that would have been, it is also highly unlikely that a cricket ball struck the fatal blow or, in fact, that there was a fatal blow struck at *all*. None of the Hanoverian children seemed particularly robust and, as can be seen elsewhere in this volume early death was far from unusual within this particular ruling house.

In a sad coda to this sorry tale, George II appeared little moved by the loss of his child. Although he did his best to help Frederick's widow in the months that followed, for his own lost son he shed no tears. Perhaps the years the two spent apart during Frederick's childhood had put a distance between them that was simply unbridgeable, or perhaps the constant butting of heads once the prince arrived in England made a bad situation worse. Whatever the cause, for George II, it seemed to be business as usual and when Frederick was laid to rest in Westminster Abbey, one might be forgiven for barely noticing at all.

The Prince Who Died of a Broken Heart

Prince Augustus William of Prussia (Hohenzollern)

Berlin, Prussia, 9 August 1722–Oranienburg, Prussia, 12 June 1758

It can sometimes be hard being the younger sibling of a golden child, the brother or sister who seems to make a success of everything they try. Seemingly with the slightest possible effort they are the first to pass each milestone, to blaze the trail that others can only follow. Spare a thought then for Augustus William of Prussia, the younger brother of none other than Frederick the Great. If being the brother of anyone successful can be a burden to bear, imagine the pressure when your sibling is so feted as Frederick... that must have seemed like an impossible act to follow.

Of course, to feel such pressure one must actually have the ambition to follow that illustrious figure in the first place and, happily, such matters were not of interest to Augustus. It is fortunate indeed, that he was not a young man who dreamt of keeping up with his siblings, especially when one learns that he was brother not only of Frederick the Great, but of the enormously ambitious Louise Ulrika of Prussia too.

With Frederick and Louise Ulrika flying the flag of absolutist power for the house of Hohenzollern, Augustus did not seek office and was perfectly content to live a quiet life behind the throne. Though politically unambitious, he did enjoy a distinguished military career, and it was a rare error of judgement on the battlefield that resulted in the collapse of his relationship with Frederick.

Augustus won the ire of his brother thanks to a disastrous showing at the Battle of Kolin during the Seven Years' War when, believing he had no other sensible option, he commanded his forces to retreat. The letters the siblings exchanged after the battle reflect the fraught situation between them from

Frederick's very first words of 'your ill conduct has very much injured my affairs'.[35] Though the letter closes with an expression of affection, it is a litany of complaints about the strategic decisions of Augustus and hit the younger man with a body blow.

Augustus was badly hurt by his argument with Frederick and though relations thawed a little, they were never full reconciled. Twelve months after the battle, Augustus took to his bed and died of a brain tumour at just thirty-five. To the public, however, the routine diagnosis was not a satisfactory explanation for such an unexpected death. Instead they put the blame down to heartache, caused by his brother's fury. Though untrue, the accusation stuck, leaving Augustus remembered as the prince who died of a broken heart.

A Fatal Toilet

George II, King of Great Britain and Ireland (Hanover)
Hanover, Holy Roman Empire, 9 November 1683–
London, England, 25 October 1760

After more than thirty years on the throne, the once vibrant George II had, as all must do, slowed considerably. With age came infirmity and as the fire of his youth dimmed, the king retired from the active political life he once lived, and even his famously hot-temper perhaps quelled just a little. The promise made at the deathbed of his adored wife, Caroline of Ansbach, had been kept and the king had not remarried following her death more than two decades earlier. In those long years, there had been mistresses, of course, yet none could fill the very precious place that Caroline once occupied and despite the many years that had passed since her death, George still mourned Caroline's loss. He had not been a faithful husband, of course, George III was the only one of our Georges who might lay claim to *that*, but old age brought with it regret.

Perhaps the silence where Caroline had once been was particularly deep in the later years of his life when solitude replaced society, failing health overtaking youthful vivacity. As is so often the case, age played a cruel trick on the monarch and his intellectual faculties remained undimmed, leaving him all too aware of the creeping loss of his sight and hearing.

Well into his seventies, it was hardly surprising that George had become a creature of habit and on the morning of his death he left his bed in Kensington Palace at 6.00 am as was his routine, seeing in the day with his usual cup of chocolate. Suitably refreshed, he retired to perform his toilet in private, leaving his valet to wait for his return. Just minutes after the king had departed there came a noise from within the toilet that sent his valet running to his master's aid, where he was greeted with an unhappy sight.

The king had fallen and was on the floor, and was barely alive. As he was carried to bed and settled as well as could be, word was sent to summon George's physician, Frank Nicholls. Princess Amelia was also sent for yet, by the time she reached her father's side, the king was dead.

Nicholls made preparations to embalm the late monarch and found that the cause of death had been an aortic dissection. Quick, painful and inevitable, no action could have been taken to prevent this massive coronary catastrophe. According to his wishes, George was buried beside his beloved Caroline at Westminster Abbey on 11 November 1760. He had longed for the day when he might be reunited with his wife, and in death his wish was granted, as the sides of their coffins were removed to allow their bodies to rest together for eternity.

Death is Just a Word

Elizabeth, Empress and Autocrat of All the Russias (Romanov)
Moscow, Russia, 29 December 1709–
St Petersburg, Russia, 5 January 1762

All of us have our own approaches to dealing with illness. Some, perhaps most, turn to doctors for help whilst others look to more alternative remedies. A few even prefer to tell themselves that all is well. After all, if one doesn't think about the worst, then the worst might not happen. Empress Elizabeth of Russia was one such woman and, as January dawned in 1762, she had little to celebrate in the state of her own health but she was damned if she was going to admit it.

Elizabeth, the daughter of Peter the Great, seized the crown after orchestrating a bloodless coup in 1741 that sent a child to a prison from which he never emerged, a fate that is dealt with elsewhere in these pages. To her credit, Elizabeth kept a promise that she would sanction no death sentences during her reign, though one might argue that the solitary half-life that Ivan endured was a more brutal punishment than simple death. This new approach to sentencing only added to her popularity amongst her people as, after two decades on the Russian throne she *still* enjoyed the love of the nation. Elizabeth was respected for her refusal to capitulate to the policies of Prussia and the certainty with which she steered the country through the Seven Years' War, usually with a drink in her hand and a feast on the table.

However, all the grandeur and political success in the world are of little import when the time comes to depart this mortal coil, and things were no different for Elizabeth, whose hard-partying lifestyle was bound to end in trouble. As she entered her fiftieth year, the empress became aware that her health was failing, as increasingly violent attacks of dizziness leaving her reeling. At first she ploughed on but as her dizzy spells became more frequent and debilitating, the court physicians were summoned to tend to their monarch.

They took one look at Elizabeth, a woman of 50 who had lived a life of excess, and decided that she was suffering from nothing more worrying than the menopause. In order to ease her discomfort they might, they mused, undertake a course of treatments and offered the far from tempting possibilities of bleeding and the occasional enema but Elizabeth, to whom all talk of illness was anathema, was having none of it.

Instead, the empress soldiered on, coping as well as she could with her ailments and unaware that she was being treated anyway, the medications concealed in the sweet treats with which she comforted herself. Despite or perhaps because of her decision to maintain her duties, Elizabeth became increasingly paranoid about the fate that awaited her, even going so far as to forbid her courtiers to use the word death in her presence, lest saying it hastened its arrival. Ironically, her constant preoccupation with her physical health took a toll on her mental wellbeing and eventually the feasts and liveliness that had characterized Elizabeth's reign were a thing of the past, the empress passing her days in silent, lonely contemplation.

Of course, forbidding discussion of death and avoiding medical treatment are not appropriate remedies for illness and the ailing empress declined further as the winter of 1761 deepened. Eventually confined to her bed, she made her confession and gathered her most trusted friends to her, finally passing away on 5 January 1762. After more than a month of lying in state, Empress Elizabeth of Russia was laid to rest whilst many miles away, the boy she condemned to a life behind bars neared his second decade of incarceration.

One Semla Too Many

Adolf Frederick, King of Sweden (Holstein-Gottorp)
Gottorp, Schleswig, 14 May 1710–
Stockholm, Sweden, 12 February 1771

In 1771, the monarch of Sweden sat down to a meal that, as the saying goes, really *was* fit for a king. A well-liked man if a somewhat weak ruler, he was a chap who did not really believe in moderation. In fact, there was nothing Adolf Frederick enjoyed more in his almost two decade reign than a good feed and whilst some monarchs fell victim to assassins, others to guillotines, and one to mushrooms, in Adolf Frederick's case, it was the puddings that killed him!

On 12 February 1771, Adolf Frederick was hungry… not just peckish, but famished and, with the enthusiasm one might expect of an eighteenth century monarch, when he sat down to eat, he really made a meal of it. As the hours drew on, he tucked into lobster, caviar, sauerkraut and kippers, the seemingly endless procession of food barely slowing as the hours passed. The ravenous monarch washed these main courses down with glass after glass of champagne. Yet for every plate that he cleared, Adolf Frederick still had room for more.

One of the king's favourite sweets was a dessert known as semla, a sweet roll popular in Scandinavia and Eastern Europe. Most diners would content themselves with one or, with a very sweet tooth, maybe two but at Adolf's last meal, the king rather over-indulged in this particular treat caring nothing for the fact that it was Lent. Luckily, because the other semla fans in Sweden were observing the Lenten period, it meant that there were plenty of pastries left for the gluttonous Adolf to devour.

And devour them he did.

To finish his meal, Adolf wanted semlas… lots of semlas; fourteen portions served in hot milk, to be exact. Once the greedy king was finally sated, he retired to his chambers where he complained, perhaps unsurprisingly, of digestive pains. Adolf died that same day; whether his last meal contributed to his demise we cannot be certain, but posterity has recorded Adolf as the king who ate himself to death, the victim of one semla too many.

A Masquerade to Remember

Gustav III, King of Sweden (Holstein-Gottorp)
Stockholm, Sweden, 24 January 1746–
Stockholm, Sweden, 29 March 1792

Early in the evening of 16 March 1792, the cream of Swedish society gathered at the Royal Opera House in Stockholm to attend a masked ball. Amid the dazzling costumes and melodic music one man stood out despite the mask that concealed his identity, the dazzling star of the Royal Order of the Seraphim worn proudly on his breast. King Gustav III was a man who was used to being the centre of attention and he intended for everyone to know that their monarch was moving among them.

With nothing on his mind save for enjoying the party, Gustav met friends and settled for a private dinner in the Opera House. As wine flowed and food fit for a king was devoured, Gustav and his friends intended to let the party get underway before they graced the guests with their presence. There was perhaps a hint of the trouble to come when the meal was briefly interrupted by the arrival of a messenger who carried with him a death threat, which would be enough to put most people off their hors d'oeuvres.

The note was written in French and Gustav, setting aside his plate, took a moment to read it. He received the missive with stunning sang froid but then, this was not the first such message the king had received in his forty-six years. Utterly untroubled by the threat of violence, Gustav set the note aside and went back to his revelry. Finally, with dinner digested and all set for fun, the monarch joined the party, which was by now in full swing.

The king had barely hit the dance floor when a party of five men surrounded him with something other than his dance card on their minds. With their identities concealed behind black masks, as the men greeted the monarch, Jacob Johan Anckarström drew a pistol and shot Gustav once in the back. The gun was loaded with a deadly cocktail of balls, nails, scrap lead and iron and the contents emptied themselves into the king's body at point blank range. He staggered yet, through some admirable strength of will, remained on his feet.

As panic erupted, the wounded king was rushed from the scene of the crime and into the hands of his doctors. By dawn the following morning the attackers were in custody and they soon succumbed to interrogation and implicated their co-conspirators, whilst Anckarström himself would eventually be executed. It seemed at first that Gustav had actually managed to cheat the conspirators and that he might survive the attempt on his life. Despite the scrap ammunition, the wound was not fatal and under the watchful eye of the court doctors, it was expected that the king would live.

For almost two weeks Gustav tried to continue as head of state, determined to show his attackers that they had inflicted naught but a scratch. Fate, however, had a final twist to take and far from recovering, the king unexpectedly began to weaken. The ammunition of scrap lead and metal caused the wound to turn septic, a deadly infection setting in.

As the days drew on and the king suffered the treatments and interventions of his doctors, the wound grew ever more infected. Exhausted by his injury and the pressure of performing his court duties, the fatally weakened Gustav was easy prey to pneumonia, the infection that would succeed where his assassins had failed.

On 29 March Gustav's life reached its final hours and with his dying breath he murmured, 'A few moments rest would do me good.' Those were the last words King Gustav III would ever speak and he died soon afterwards, less than a fortnight after the fateful, fatal ball.

'I die innocent'

Louis XVI, King of France and Navarre (Bourbon)

Versailles, France, 23 August 1754–

Paris, France, 21 January 1793

Louis Auguste de France, Duke of Berry, had come a long way from those early years when his parents, Louis, the Dauphin of France, and Maria Josepha of Saxony, barely noticed the quiet little boy so eclipsed by his charming, short-lived elder brother. The timid and unassuming child who once nursed that same brother through his final illness had grown, if not blossomed into an equally timid man. No longer a boy, he was now a father and husband to the Habsburg Archduchess Maria Antonia, better known to history as Marie Antoinette. Both husband and wife would, of course, die on the guillotine but before we join him on the scaffold, let us learn more of how he came to be there.

In 1774 that shy young man who had never expected to be king, found himself thrust onto the throne of France as Louis XVI. Utterly overwhelmed and underprepared despite his education in all matters monarchical, Louis proved to be a fatally indecisive ruler, desperate to be liked by the people even as he allowed himself to be influenced by his ministers and advisers in matters of policy of state. A series of unpopular policy decisions at home and abroad knocked the new monarch's confidence and, with the government descending deeper and deeper into debt, Louis found himself not waving, but drowning.

As the high-living royal household was seen as profligate and wasteful, down in the rural fields and city streets, the people of France were finding life increasingly difficult. With food costs soaring, corruption among the ruling classes rife and forays into the Seven Years' War and the American War of Independence proving ruinously expensive, Louis prevaricated over financial reform at a moment when decisive action was needed. He turned to Jacques Necker to sort out the fiscal mess into which the nation was descending but Necker would not enjoy influence for long and soon faced a somewhat less literal chop. This proved to be a catastrophic misjudgement and the dismissal of this hugely popular man of the people would eventually play a part in the iconic fall of the Bastille, a pivotal moment in the French Revolution.

The public weren't only taxed to the limit, they were starving too and famine swept the country in the 1780s, leaving death and misery in its terrible wake. A cloud of dissent swirled across the land and the masses turned their gaze on the opulent splendour of Versailles, where they saw profligacy and decadence. Whipped up by pamphleteers and naysayers, they mocked and jeered a king who had completely lost touch with the subjects he ruled.

France was, the people believed, led by a king who could not or would not imagine what the lives of his subjects were like, preferring instead to live in a decadent bubble. His wife was draped in the latest fashions, his household filled with the finest luxuries available and while the people starved, the court dined on fine food. Louis was not so out of touch that he did not notice his waning popularity, and he looked once more to his advisors, hoping for a solution to magically appear. Instead, influential and ambitious nobles and politicians jockeyed to take advantage of his indecisive, quiet nature and Louis let himself be led straight down the path of public derision.

Bowing to the wishes of his advisors, the king faltered when it came to matters of reform and in 1789, he summoned the Estates-General, seeking guidance on taxation policy. The Estates-General was an assembly made up of the different estates of France: the clergy (the First Estate), the nobles (the Second Estate), and the people (the Third Estate). Furious at their exclusion from the meeting in the Hôtel des Menus Plaisirs in Versailles, members of the Third Estate held a conference on a nearby tennis court. They believed that they were deliberately refused entry to the king's meeting and swore an oath of allegiance that they would not disband until a French constitution was written. Whether the doors were locked to keep them out or simply to mark the royal family's deep mourning for the heir to the throne, Louis Joseph, Dauphin of France, who had been dead barely a fortnight is debatable, but the die was cast and the Tennis Court Oath was a turning point as French citizens formally declared their opposition to the monarch. Faced with this vote of no-confidence, Louis attempted to make concessions but the damage was done. Now the idea of a new constitution took root among the citizens; within the month there were mobs on the streets of Paris and on 14 July 1789, the Bastille fell.

Four years before he mounted the scaffold, the path that would lead Louis to the grave was already beginning to take shape in the dissent of the French people and politicians and his ever-loosening grip on royal authority. Fearing for his future and with talks going nowhere, the royal family set in place plans to flee for Montmédy and the protection of Austria. If he could but escape France and virtual house arrest and see his wife and children safe, Louis hoped that he might one day return with the backing of a military force culled from sympathetic nations and reassert monarchial authority. However, indecision struck the king again and he postponed the escape multiple times, not quite able to let go of the hope that the people would come round, the politicians would settle and all would once again be well.

When the family did finally undertake what has become known as the flight to Varennes in June 1791, the plan was doomed to failure. Apparently recognizing Louis from his portrait on a coin, a local man, Jean-Baptiste Drouet, raised the alarm and the last chance of freedom was lost. There would be no further opportunity for escape; instead the royal family was returned to the Tuileries and placed under arrest once more.

Looking to his fellow European monarchs for salvation, Louis found himself met by a wall of platitudinous concern but precious little in the way of real action. Declarations were issued, sabres were rattled and fingers were wagged, but nobody rode to his rescue, the white chargers remaining resolutely stabled. France now found that it had few friends on the continent and one can only imagine how Louis must have felt as he watched his last remaining chances for escape slipping away, the family he loved growing more isolated with each passing day. When the Tuileries was stormed by a mob and the royal family was escorted out of the palace to the Legislative Assembly, their already restricted world shrank even further.

The quiet, gentle man who had once sat on the throne of France was arrested on 13 August 1792 and sent with his family to the Temple, a Parisian prison that would be his final home. Just over a month later the National Convention abolished the Monarchy, declaring France a Republic and the former king nothing grander that *Citoyen Louis Capet*. As his opponents were now to find, abolishing a monarchy was one thing but there remained the problem of what to do with the man who had presided over it. Debate now began in earnest over his future. There were precious few options available and whilst the moderates strongly encouraged the continued imprisonment of Louis or even his possible exile, radical voices argued that nothing less than death would satisfy justice.

Once again, the politicians debated as politicians are so wont to do until, on 11 December 1792, Louis and his counsel, Raymond Romain, Count de Sèze, appeared before the Convention to hear charges of high treason and crimes against the State. Just over a month later, on 15 January 1793, a dignified Louis listened as the verdict of guilty was read out against him. He was sentenced to death and returned to the Temple, his appointment with the executioner scheduled for 21 January 1793.

On the last evening of his life, Louis said his farewells to his family. More than anything he wished to spare his children the agony of knowing they would never see their father again and he promised he would visit in the morning, a meeting that he knew could not happen. At dawn on the day of his execution the former king celebrated mass and then, all hope of mercy gone, prepared to journey by carriage to the scaffold where a crowd of thousands waited to see their version of justice enacted.

When Louis left his bed at 5.00 am, he was greeted by a rainswept, miserable day. No doubt his wife and children were on his mind as he passed the early hours in contemplation and prayer until a steady stream of visitors began to arrive. The former king was taken from the Temple at around 8.00 am to be met by over 1000 horse guards who had been appointed to escort the prisoner on the long journey from the prison to the place of execution in the Place de la Révolution. Unlike Marie Antoinette's final, unhappy journey later that year, Louis was afforded the dignity of a closed carriage and he asked if he might be accompanied by Father Henry Essex Edgeworth, an Irish priest.

During the carriage ride Louis remained utterly composed, praying with Father Edgeworth and apparently untroubled by the vast crowds of citizens who lined the route, any sound they might make drowned by innumerable drummers who walked ahead of the procession. The former Place Louis XV had once been a place that celebrated the splendour of the Bourbon monarchy, but now it would witness its final moments.

At the end of the two hour carriage ride, Louis climbed from the vehicle to gaze upon the scaffold that towered above the crowd of around 20,000 spectators. As guards gathered around him he politely dismissed any notion that they would be the ones to prepare him for his fate and begged leave to do so himself. With steady hands he untied his own neckerchief, opened the collar of his shirt and declared himself ready to proceed. Momentarily stilled by such a composed display, the guards recovered themselves and moved to bind his hands, at which point Louis pointedly refuted their efforts, their very audacity distasteful to him even in these desperate final minutes.

Taking the arm of the priest who had ridden with him, Louis passed along the unmade path to the scaffold as the citizens of Paris looked on, gathered to witness a truly momentous occasion. As he mounted the steps, the king who had been undone by timidity finally sparked into life, addressing those who had gathered to watch his execution with these words:

> 'I die innocent of all the crimes laid to my charge; I pardon those who have occasioned my death; and I pray to God that the blood you are going to shed may never be visited on France.'[36]

At that, the drummers picked up their sticks and resumed their rhythmic beat. Again the crowd roared its approval, urging the guards on as they seized the former king and set him beneath the blade that was under the control of executioner, Charles-Henri Sanson. With no further ceremony the National Razor fell, ending the life of Louis XVI at just after 10.15 am to the sound of a furious, deafening thunder of celebration from the crowd. Fired up by their excitement, one of the guards seized the late king's head and promenaded around the scaffold. Yet at this stark, grisly image, the multitude fell suddenly silent, perhaps realizing for the first time the enormity of the moments they had just witnessed, when a nation changed forever in the blink of an eye. Presently though cries of support could be heard until the streets rang with shouts of, 'Vive la République!'.

The body of the former king was taken for burial in the churchyard of the Church of the Madeleine, where he lay until 1815. At the restoration of the Bourbon monarchy, Louis and Marie Antoinette's remains were retrieved and interred in the Basilica of Saint-Denis, their memories honoured by a monument to their passing.

'My blood alone remains'

Marie Antoinette, Queen of France and Navarre (Bourbon)

Vienna, Austria, 2 November 1755–
Paris, France, 16 October 1793

In the darkest hours of 16 October 1793, the inmates of La Conciergerie slumbered on their meagre beds, snatching a few hours of escape from their terrible surroundings and the grim fates that awaited them. These were the prisoners of the French Revolution, stripped of name, robbed of dignity, and condemned to a public death.

One of their number did not sleep and deep within the walls of the notorious prison a now-legendary widow waited for her last sunrise, torn from her children and family and thrust from a life of privilege into one of penury and despair.

Like many a condemned prisoner before her, this particular convict was known by many names. Court papers know her as Prisoner 280 whilst to those who presided over her arrest, she was the widow Capet. History, of course, has remembered her by the very title that the Revolutionary Tribunal sought to expunge and the name of Marie Antoinette, Queen of France and Navarre, has become iconic, symbolic of tragedy, romance and privilege run rampant.

The show trial that condemned Prisoner 280 had been vicious and exhausting, the charges laid at her feet ranging from treason to incest and deep into the night it continued, the former queen speaking only sparingly as the final act of her life raged on. Yet for all of the theatre and drama of the courtroom there was little doubt as to the eventual outcome and the sentence that set her date with the guillotine was little more than a legal formality. As far as the prosecutors were concerned, Marie Antoinette was to follow her husband, Louis XVI, into an unmarked grave.

The humble cell that was now Marie Antoinette's home was a world away from the splendour she had once known, the queen's vibrant life reduced to a lonely existence of prayer and contemplation. Crushed by the execution of her husband after nearly a quarter of a century of marriage, Marie Antoinette had clung to the remains of her ill-fated family until she was ripped from their arms and now, in the closing hours of her life, she was to know little comfort.

Scant hours had passed since the former queen had been found guilty of treason by the Revolutionary Tribunal. Her sentence had been read at around 4.00 am that same morning and before the next sunset she would die beneath the keen blade of the National Razor. With no right of appeal and nothing to be gained from pleading for mercy, the condemned woman was taken to her cell to await the new day and her date with Henri Sanson, the executioner whose father had operated the guillotine that ended the life of the late king.

As we have seen, when Louis went to the guillotine not even a year earlier, he had been afforded a measure of dignity in his final hours but for his widow, this was not to be the case. In poor health and suffering from menstrual haemorrhaging that hinted at a far more serious condition, she sat up into the night and wrote a final, heartfelt letter to Madame Élisabeth, her sister-in-law. Within its pages, the condemned former queen implored Élisabeth to care for the children who would be left behind. The tear-stained missive never reached its recipient and within the year Élisabeth too would die on the guillotine. With her letter finished, Marie Antoinette penned a few final lines in her prayer book, which would later be found among the papers of Robespierre:

'My God, have pity on me! My eyes have no more tears to cry for you my poor children; adieu! adieu!'

The sun had not yet risen on that cold October day when Marie Antoinette was joined by her maid, Rosalie Lamorlière, newly arrived at the cell to carry out her final duties. Refused permission to wear her black widow's gown, Rosalie helped Marie Antoinette dress in a simple white cap, kerchief and dress. Under the watchful eye of the jailers, mistress and maid undertook a final toilette. When a plea was made for the men who stood by to avert their gaze so that she might change her bloodstained undergarments, the request was refused and with Rosalie's help she was forced to undress before them, doing her best to maintain what dignity remained. Newly changed and washed, Marie Antoinette attempted to swallow a few spoonfuls of soup to appease her retainer but could barely bring herself to face the simple food and it was a downcast Rosalie who took her leave, as her mistress returned once more to her prayers.

After the long, dark night the dawning rays of the sun brought no respite to Marie Antoinette and as day broke over Paris, she received a procession of formal visitors, all keen to play their role in these final hours. Prison and court officials filed into the cell to carry out their administrative duties and a priest arrived to hear any last confession, a service that the condemned woman refused. Eventually the door opened to admit Sanson, marking the start of preparations for the guillotine.

Marie Antoinette's hair was cut short and her hands bound and the woman who had once traveled in the finest style known to France was taken to Cour du Mai where a tumbrel awaited to carry her to her fate. Calmly, she protested that her late husband, Louis XVI, had made his last journey in a closed carriage, protected from the crowds who gathered to watch him pass but the officials coldly told the prisoner that times had changed since then, it was her fate to face the people of Paris head on.

Accompanied by a sworn priest, Sanson and his assistant, and travelling a route heavy with security, Marie Antoinette endured the ride to the scaffold in dignified silence. In the final sketch of her, hastily drawn by master propagandist Jacques-Louis David, we see a woman aged beyond her years yet dignified and strong, sitting straight-backed on her way to meet her fate.

As the mob heckled and jeered she showed no fear, maintaining her dignity until, at the sight of the towering guillotine in Place de la Révolution, her composure momentarily faltered. With the catcalls of the crowd rising to a deafening roar Marie Antoinette gathered herself, stepped down from the tumbrel as though she were stepping from the finest coach and calmly ascended the steps to the scaffold.

From that point on Marie Antoinette did not falter in her composure again. She made no effort to acknowledge the crowd and said her last words, 'I did not do it on purpose'[37] to her executioner, offering a gentle apology for stepping lightly on his foot as she crossed the scaffold.

As her late husband once faced the guillotine with composed dignity, so too did his queen go to the National Razor with no trace of the anguish that she must surely have felt. Fifteen minutes after noon the blade thundered down and the woman known to those who loathed her as widow Capet and those who loved her as the queen of France, was dead.

The crowd roared its approval as her decapitated head was displayed to them, the curtain call of this most macabre piece of street theatre. Marie Antoinette's body was thrown into an unmarked grave in the Madeleine cemetery and there it would remain until 1815, when the late queen and king's remains were exhumed and interred at the Basilica of St Denis.

Marie Antoinette's life was one of wild contrasts, of flamboyant highs and terrible lows. Perhaps more than any other woman in history she has been lionized and demonized, revered as a martyr and loathed as a traitor and yet at the last she was simply a bereaved wife terrified for the fate of her soon to be orphaned children. Whether royalist or revolutionary, one cannot deny that Marie Antoinette showed dignity to the end, regal in every sense of the word.

'I beg you take courage'

Catherine II, Empress and Autocrat of all the Russias, known as Catherine the Great (Romanov)

Stettin, Prussia, 2 May 1729–
St Petersburg, Russia, 17 November 1796

More than two centuries after her death, Catherine the Great remains one of the most iconic and recognizable rulers in the history of the world. Immensely powerful, well-respected and hugely influential, her reign spanned more than a quarter of a century and her place in history is assured, if always accompanied by a little equine balderdash. Strong and seemingly immovable, in 1796 Catherine finally encountered an obstacle that she could not overcome, when the Grim Reaper came to call during the St Petersburg winter.

By 1796 the Empress and Autocrat of all the Russias was 67-years-old and as the decades of intrigue and drama rolled on, her robust health finally began to fail. Although Catherine was as vibrant and committed to her rule as she had ever been, physically she was slowing down, and her court could see it as well as the lady herself.

Still, there was nothing out of the ordinary that might cause concern when Catherine retired to her bed on 15 November 1796. In fact she slept soundly through the night and rose early as she always did, welcoming the new day with her usual cup of coffee and a chat with her maid, Maria Perekusikhina.

With Maria happily engaged in her duties, Catherine went through to her study to begin the business of the day and settled with her correspondence, a regular habit for an empress as committed as she was. A most dedicated sort of lady, Catherine liked to get her admin out of the way early and at just 9.00 am, she went to her dressing room to perform her toilette and no doubt reflect on a morning already well spent.

Well-used to the familiar routine of the empress, it struck her chamberlain, Zakhar Zotov, that Catherine had been in her closet for an unusually long time and he took an executive decision to interrupt the royal ablutions. He opened the door just a little to enquire as to Catherine's wellbeing and found his mistress collapsed on the floor, her face a worrying shade of purple. The empress was utterly insensible, her pulse and breathing dangerously weak, and as Zotov watched, she slipped into unconsciousness.

Under the watchful eye of the loyal Zotov, servants were summoned to lift Catherine and carry her to the bedroom, where they made her as comfortable as they were able. Within the hour Catherine's Scottish physician, Doctor John Rogerson, arrived and performed an examination. His diagnosis was stark, certain and accurate: the Empress of Russia had suffered a massive stroke and would not recover.

Whilst the courtiers of the Winter Palace buzzed about in a panic, Rogerson made fruitless efforts to revive his royal patient yet even as he bled her and did what little he could, her condition only worsened. Disturbing spasms and violent seizures wracked Catherine's body, she vomited worrying quantities of blood and by the evening she had fallen into a coma from which she would never awake. Her son (and later victim of an assassination attempt), Grand Duke Paul, set up residence in his mother's chambers to prepare for the inevitable politicking that would accompany his succession. He was in constant contact with the doctors tending her and when they confirmed that all hope was lost, Paul requested that his mother receive the last rites.

As 17 November 1796 drew on, the rooms of the empress were a flurry of activity and doctors, priests, bishops and courtiers came and went.

Some visited Paul, some paid their respects and others were there in their professional capacity, but each and every one was awaiting the news that the palace was dreading. With Rogerson in near-constant attendance, Catherine was made as comfortable as was possible for a woman in her final hours and at 9.45 pm, surrounded by her dearest friends and loyal courtiers, she took her last breath.

As she had lived her life in opulence, so too was Catherine the Great to meet her maker in fine style. Cared for in death as she was in life by her closest and most loyal ladies-in-waiting, the late empress was dressed in silver brocade, her priceless crown placed on her head. She was laid in state in the chamber of mourning, created by Antonio Rinaldi, the Italian architect who had made his name during her reign. As the court and people paid their respects, Catherine the Great was laid to rest at the Peter and Paul Cathedral in St Petersburg, her reign finally at an end.

Bloody Murder in St Petersburg

Paul I, Emperor and Autocrat of All the Russias (Romanov)
St Petersburg, Russia, 1 October 1754–
St Petersburg, Russia, 23 March 1801

With childbirth, revolutionaries and overeager physicians just a few of the hazards waiting to send the crowned heads of Europe in the eighteenth century to their graves, one might be forgiven for hoping that our regal subjects could at least trust their own courtiers and families. One might *hope* that, but then one might also be in for as rude an awakening as Emperor Paul I of Russia received in the fifth year of his reign, when he discovered that the adage of keeping your friends close and your enemies closer was truer than he might have guessed.

During his short tenure Paul made powerful and influential enemies thanks to his strongly held and, to us, quite reasonable beliefs that the noble classes should behave in a chivalrous and honourable fashion. Indeed, he further blotted his copybook by attempting to put in place measures to fight corruption in the highest government offices, which did not endear him to those in authority. Not content to upset some of the most influential figures in Russia, he compounded the issue by increasing rights for poorer citizens and establishing new laws that ensured the most impoverished estate workers could expect better treatment from their employers. All of these moves are laudable, of course, but they are also calculated to annoy the sort of powerful people who do not take kindly to seeing the applecart nudged, let alone upset.

Paul was well aware of how his reforms would go down and he lived in fear that each day would be his last, convinced that an assassin would eventually strike him down. His fears were to prove devastatingly well-founded thanks to a conspiracy of noblemen including Counts Pyotr Alekseyevich Pahlen, Nikolay Zubov and Nikita Petrovich Panin, as well as Admiral José de Ribas, who died before the assassination could be carried out.

As the night of 23 March 1801 fell, Paul hosted a dinner party in St Michael's Castle at which he was joined by his son, Grand Duke Alexander, who did not appear to enjoy the company of his father that evening. Paul eventually retired to his bedroom as elsewhere, the conspirators waited for the appointed hour to carry out their grim task. They passed the evening together drinking until they were admitted to the castle by a member of staff who had been recruited to their cause. Safely inside, the group made their way swiftly to the emperor's chambers where they easily overwhelmed domestic staff as Pahlen hurried to Alexander's room to wait for the gruesome deed to be carried out.

Hearing a commotion in the hallway as the assassins clashed with his guards, the terrified Paul took refuge behind a screen. As he cowered, General Levin August, Count von Bennigsen, and Prince Vladimir Mikhailovich Yashvil burst into the chamber with their supporters and, finding the bed empty, turned the room over and dragged the terrified man from his hiding place. At knifepoint Paul was forced to sit at his desk and they instructed him to sign abdication papers, which he refused to do. No amount of threats or coercion could convince Paul to bow to this demand and when he tried to resist, he was struck with the blade of a sword by one of the band and viciously attacked. In the ensuing chaos, the emperor was strangled to death with a scarf and beaten viciously by his attackers. So did the reign of Paul I end in violence and Alexander I rise unchecked to power.

None of the conspirators faced severe punishment for their part in the plot and Pahlen's influence and reach ensured that much of the conspiracy remained mired in mystery for many years. The question of whether Alexander was involved in his father's murder has never been satisfactorily settled, despite several valiant efforts to untangle the conspiracy and his possible place in it. Perhaps he knew of the plot, perhaps he believed a peaceful abdication was the aim or perhaps he was utterly innocent and knew nothing of the assassination beforehand. Whatever the truth of the matter, the new emperor always felt a sense of shame for winning the throne through his father's violent death and later developed a paranoia that his own life might be threatened, a worry that would plague the final years of his reign.

Death of a Devoted Consort

Charlotte of Mecklenburg-Strelitz, Queen of the United Kingdom of Great Britain and Ireland (Hanover)

Mirow, Holy Roman Empire, 19 May 1744–
Kew, England, 17 November 1818

There can be few royal consorts as devoted as Charlotte of Mecklenburg-Strelitz, wife of George III. From the heady early days of their union in 1761, Charlotte was a loving and faithful spouse and her husband rejected the royal tradition of taking mistresses, happy in the company of his quiet, graceful queen. Throughout the long years of their marriage, with all the well-documented health problems both physical and mental that George suffered, Charlotte remained his loving and most protective companion. Though her devotion to her king was arguably detrimental to the marriage ambitions of her daughters is a point to consider, one cannot doubt that she acted in the best interests of her husband. Once the king's frailty left him unable to rule and the regency was established, Charlotte remained his closest advisor and carer yet she was not, of course, immortal.

As the queen entered her seventy-fourth year, she was notably fragile. Her husband's tenuous mental health had seen him confined to Windsor Castle and though she tried her best to continue with her official duties, it was apparent to all who saw her that Charlotte was in poor health. Her last public engagement came in April of 1818 when, with a typically low-key approach, she visited the Mansion House to attend a prize-giving ceremony in honour of the National Society for Promoting the Education of the Poor.

Following that last philanthropic engagement Charlotte gathered her daughters, Mary and Augusta to her and took up residence at Dutch House. Away from the bustle of official duties, the queen still hoped that she might recover her health enough to travel on to Windsor to join her husband and daughter, Sophia, but it was not to be. In fact, far from growing stronger, her health declined at a rapid rate. Hidden away from the public gaze with only her adult children for company, Charlotte suffered terribly. Her legs swelled and her joints grew sore and gangrenous until she could barely move at all.

The ailing queen's immobility contributed to her worsening health and as the year drew on she contracted pneumonia, the final illness of her eventful life. On 17 November 1818 Charlotte settled in a comfortable armchair, her children at her side. With her frail hand held safely in that of her son, the Prince Regent, the queen passed quietly away. Only in death did she make that longed for trip to Windsor, where she was laid to rest. King George III, suffering from dementia, never learnt of his beloved wife's death and followed her to the grave less than eighteen months later.

A Tragic Mother

Maria Isabel, Queen of Spain (Braganza)

Queluz, Portugal, 19 May 1797–

Madrid, Spain, 26 December 1818

With guillotines, gangrene, hernias and more, the list of threats to the lives of our European royals in the eighteenth century is nothing if not varied and to that we must add childbirth. Death in childbirth was sadly not uncommon but there is a gruesome surgical twist to the last moments of Maria Isabel of Portugal that is not for the faint of heart.

As the daughter of John VI of Portugal and his wife, Carlota Joaquina of Spain, the young infanta's parents always intended that she would have a vital part to play in the European marriage market. To their eye, the ideal candidate appeared to be Maria Isabel's maternal uncle, Ferdinand VII, who was to acquire something of a hobby for marrying his nieces. Worries about inbreeding and familial relations were nowhere on the horizon and after a decade as a widower with no heir, the King of Spain was in need of a young, childbearing wife.

The royal wedding took place on 29 September 1816, with the 19-year-old bride married to her 31-year-old uncle and set for a life in Spain. Perhaps contrary to what one might expect given their familial relationship, this was a royal marriage that got off to a happy start and the couple found one another diverting company even if they weren't quite madly in love. Given how some of our royal marriages played out, diverting company is a positively ringing endorsement and the respective families were delighted when, just a few months into the marriage, news reached them that the longed-for heir was finally on the way. To all intents and purposes, it seemed that things were rosy in Spain, the purpose of the marriage well on track to being accomplished.

Sadly the happiness of the couple was short-lived and though they welcomed a daughter, María Luisa Isabel, in August 1817, she lived barely five months before her premature death plunged the new parents into mourning. The Spanish court once again waited with baited breath for their heir, and once again an official pregnancy announcement was made but, as you might have guessed, the story was not destined to end happily.

Maria Isabel went into labour in December 1818; long, agonizing hours passed as she tried without success to deliver a stillborn, breeched baby. Having suffered prolonged seizures during the delivery, the queen lapsed into a coma so deep that the royal physicians believed she was dead and immediately began to cut into their patient with the intention of removing her deceased daughter. In fact, Maria Isabel was not dead, though she soon would be. The physicians listened with horror as the 'corpse' of the queen gave a cry of agony at the touch of their blades, the newly-cut surgical wound in her abdomen already bleeding profusely.

So comprehensive were the queen's injuries from both the difficult birth and the surgery that followed that she had no hope of survival. She died that same day, aged just 21. Her bereft husband mourned his wife deeply and built the Museo del Prado in honour of her dedication to art and antiquity, a monumental achievement that stands to this day.

The Death of Farmer George

George III, King of the United Kingdom of Great Britain and Ireland (Hanover)

London, England, 4 June 1738–
Windsor, England, 29 January 1820

When King George III breathed his last at Windsor Castle on 29 January 1820, he was a shadow of the well-loved monarch he had once been, the 'farmer' who had sat on the throne for nearly six decades, long since eclipsed by tales of madness. His health and mental wellbeing weakened beyond repair by well-publicized and incurable bouts of insanity. The king knew little of the world around him nor the family to which he had once been devoted. Charlotte, the queen who had been at his side as his nurse, lover and counsellor, had gone to her grave in 1818. Yet her husband knew nothing of her loss nor even her burial at Windsor, which had been his home since 1811. For nine years the king had been kept out of the public eye, cosseted under constant care as his fragile state grew weaker by the day.

With the passing of the Care of King During his Illness, etc. Act 1811 (ostensibly the Regency Act), George, the former Prince of Wales, was elevated to the position of Prince Regent. Free of responsibilities, the king could fade quietly into the background and, his physicians hoped, conquer his madness. Relieved of the burden of office and public life, the king's health did not recover but continued to deteriorate. As his dementia worsened and his hearing and mobility failed, the elderly king grew increasingly incoherent until he was in a state of near-permanent insanity.

The king was blinded by cataracts and crippled by rheumatic pain, his emotional state as fragile as his physical. It is perhaps merciful that he did *not* know of Charlotte's death when we consider the shock he had received at the passing of his youngest daughter, Princess Amelia, in 1810. Her death had hit the whole family with the force of a blow and for years thereafter Amelia's bereaved father would cry out to see her or, sometimes, tell people that she was married and raising her family in Hanover. In reality, Amelia had never been allowed to marry the man she adored yet in this delusional world, Amelia was forever young, beautiful and happy, captured for all time as George's ideal daughter.

With his son, Frederick, Duke of York, at his side, George III died on 29 January 1820 in Windsor Castle, the home that had become his hospital and sanctuary. Perhaps, given his suffering, one might speculate that this was a merciful release. Three weeks later he was laid to rest in St George's Chapel, Windsor Castle, mourned by the country that had loved him.

'What eye has wept for him?'

George IV, King of the United Kingdom of Great Britain and Ireland (Hanover)

London, England, 12 August 1762–
Windsor, England, 26 June 1830

Few kings have come to define an era more than the man once known as 'Prinny' or, to give him his formal name, George IV, King of the United Kingdom of Great Britain and Ireland. In his time he was Prince of Wales, Prince Regent and king, debtor, scandal-monger, gambler and gentleman of fashion, but call him what you may, from romance to politics, George IV never did anything by halves.

Any man who lives a life rich with decadence and debauchery must eventually pay the piper and after nearly seventy years of the high life, George's love of booze, banquets and bacchanalia caught up with him. On 26 June 1830, he finally ate and drank his way into the grave, leaving behind a less than enviable reputation that has loomed large over his memory. His enduring image has become that of a rouged buffoon, better remembered for the girth of his corset and his opulent lifestyle than his efforts at playing the political king. He lived out his life of unapologetic extravagance in the full gaze of press and public, a very modern sort of celebrity who fascinated and repelled in equal measure.

The pages of Georgian history are all the richer thanks to George's scandalous escapades but even the most carefree cad must eventually mature and at least attempt respectability. Accordingly, the once hard-partying king retired to the secluded chambers of Windsor Castle just as his father had before him. However, whereas George III's days had been spent in a fog of insensibility and hopeless medical treatment, his son whiled away the hours indulging his love of fine foods and finer wines. The man who had once cut such a dash through society ballooned in size until he weighed in excess of seventeen stone, his corpulent bulk squeezed into punishing corsets intended to confine a fifty-inch waist, the finely tailored contents of his wardrobe altered to conceal and flatter the ever-expanding royal girth.

Of course, such size can only wreak havoc with one's health and the young rake disappeared beneath rolls of fat that did more than ruin the outline of his tailor Louis Bazalgette's beautifully cut breeches. Under the leadership of Sir Henry Halford the king's physicians certainly earned their keep, doing battle with episodes of breathlessness so bad that George almost suffocated under the weight of his own body. Throw in aggressive attacks of gout, dropsy and any number of other problems that plagued the ailing monarch, and there could be no doubt that his time was fast approaching.

As spring gave way to summer, the health of the 67-year-old king became a source of great concern to his physicians and they decided that an extreme situation called for a response in kind. As he writhed in agony from a fresh and unexplained pain, this time one that stabbed at his bladder and lower extremities, George was plied with laudanum in futile efforts to lessen his suffering, yet still he complained. The liberal application of leeches made things no easier for the elderly king and he understandably slipped into a deep depression, tormented not only by physical pains but also by the memories of happier times that were long since passed. His melancholy was only exacerbated by the fact that the ever-worsening breathlessness left him sleepless for days on end and, despairing of ever curing these maladies, it was decided that he should take a special chair that could double as a partly upright bed and offer him at least a grain of comfort.

On his last night on earth, George retired in the company of his friend, Sir Jonathan Wathen-Waller, who was entrusted with keeping vigil beside the chair-cum-bed as the king slipped into a fitful slumber. In the early hours of 26 June 1830, the king woke in such a breathless state and suffering such incredible pain that Halford was summoned immediately from his own bed and sent to attend his employer. As the doctor hurried to the room, George gasped, 'Watty, what is this?'.[38] A moment passed in silence and he reached for Wathen-Waller's hand, telling him, 'My boy, this is death'.[39]

Though he wasn't always the most perceptive of gentlemen, on this occasion he was dead right. In the darkest hours of the morning, as the clock struck 3.15 am, the last King George of the glorious Georgian era passed away.

Of course, the Georgian gentlemen of the press were nothing if not brutally honest and the last word must belong to his now infamous obituary, published in *The Times*:

'There never was an individual less regretted by his fellow-creatures than this deceased king. What eye has wept for him? What heart has heaved one throb of unmercenary sorrow? ... If he ever had a friend — a devoted friend in any rank of life — we protest that the name of him or her has not yet reached us.'[40]

The King Who Rotted on his Throne

Louis XVIII, King of France and Navarre, known as Louis the Desired (Bourbon)

Versailles, France, 17 November 1755–
Paris, France, 16 September 1824

As we have seen on our journey through the courts of Europe, the life of Louis XVIII, the last French monarch to die on the throne, was an eventful one. From heading the court in exile in Russia to enduring the scandalous behaviour of his wife and her best friend, Louis certainly didn't have a quiet time of it. As brother of Louis XVI, Louis XVIII had never really expected to become king. The Revolution swept expectations aside and when his nephew, little Louis XVII died in prison, he was proclaimed king by the court in exile. Louis XVIII outlived his queen, Marie Joséphine of Savoy, by fourteen years and when death ended his reign he had been the official, as opposed to the self-proclaimed king for less than a decade, with a certain chap named Napoleon to thank for an unexpected interlude in his monarchy.

At the dawn of 1824, it was already apparent to those who knew Louis that he was not long for this world. With nine months to go before his appointment with the Reaper, he spent a painfully long time sliding down the slippery slope that ended alongside his illustrious ancestors interred in St Denis.

If one is being diplomatic, one might have described Louis as robust, but by the year of his death, the king's weight had ballooned out of control. His ever-expanding girth did nothing to mollify the constant agony he endured thanks to a bout of gangrene that started in his foot and progressed, unchecked and fatally, into his spine. With his mobility further hampered by an attack of gout in his extremities, the king's many and varied health conditions meant that on occasion he was barely conscious, let alone capable of ruling. Still, he had lived through the most tumultuous years in his nation's recent history and if he could survive Marie Joséphine, he was more than willing to take on death itself. After all, he was a king, chosen by God – surely something as mundane as illness could not defeat him.

As other monarchs found, the will to go on living against the odds can only carry one so far and as the year wore on, Louis became less coherent and closer to death with each passing day. As long as he could prop himself up at his desk and carry out matters of state the facade of normality might be maintained but all pretence of business as usual was abandoned when, on 12 September 1824, theatres and businesses in Paris were told to close in expectation that the king would be dead within days. Even then, Louis would not accept his inevitable fate and tried to plough on, his resolve buckling only when Zoé Talon, Countess of Cayla and the king's devoted companion, begged him to receive the last rites. This must have been a moment of devastating truth for the elderly man, to be told by the one person closest to him that the time had come to prepare for death. Now there could be no more pretence, no more self-delusion and with a heavy heart, Louis submitted to the priest's spiritual ministrations.

As the days passed without word, a crowd of citizens gathered before the Tuileries to await news of their monarch's health whilst deep within the walls of the palace, courtiers and officials crowded into the king's private rooms and counted down the hours in the company of his helpless doctors. In the splendour and peace of the palace, the stale air was foul with the stench of gangrene, the opulent environs carrying something of the whiff of the charnel house that the masses outside were, thankfully, spared.

In the middle of the afternoon on 16 September 1824, in an air thick with the scent of death, Louis XVIII took his final breath. Wracked with suffering and exhausted beyond fight, the king's already partially rotted body was embalmed, dressed in its finest garb and put on display. For a month the corpse of the king lay in state before it was interred in the Basilica of St Denis, Louis XVIII's roaming finally at an end.

Afterword

'It is our painful duty to announce the death of his Majesty, KING WILLIAM THE FOURTH, an event for which the subjects of the British Crown have for some days been in a great degree prepared. [...] His Majesty was [...] within two months of completing the seventy-second year of his age – within about three weeks of completing the nineteenth year of his marriage – and wanted but six days of having reigned seven years.'[41]

And so, with those melancholy words, ended the Georgian era.

In our journey through the royal courts of eighteenth century Europe, we have peeked in at all manner of events from birth to death and plenty in between.

Some of these events rocked nations and continue to resonate today whether in our halls of learning, ruling families or in the very make up of the continental territories and their modes of government, whilst others came and went with barely anyone noticing at all. Whatever their long-term echoes, in every case the royal houses concerned would certainly have felt the impact of those disastrous marriages, whirlwind affairs, whispered scandals or unusual deaths.

One of the most difficult aspects of writing this compendium of royal tales was deciding which to leave out. I hope that this has been a tantalizing taster of the wonders of the Georgian era and proof that, in the courts of Europe, it wasn't all powdered wigs, pomp and protocol. There was much more to life that that...

Bibliography

Adams, Jerome R. *Notable Latin American Woman*. Jefferson: McFarland & Co, 1995.

Alison, Archibald. *History of Europe from the Commencement of the French Revolution*. London: W Blackwood and Sons, 1835.

Anonymous. *The Life and Memoirs of Her Royal Highness Princess Charlotte of Saxe Coburg Saalfeld & C.* London: T. Kinnersley, 1818.

Ansimov, Evgeni V. *Five Empresses: Court Life in Eighteenth-Century Russia*. Westport: Praeger Publishers, 2004.

Aspinall, Arthur. *Letters of the Princess Charlotte 1811–1817*. London: Home & Van Thal, 1949.

Aspinall, Arthur (ed.). *Mrs Jordan and Her Family: Being the Unpublished Correspondence of Mrs Jordan and the Duke of Clarence, Later William IV.* London: Arthur Barker, 1951.

Aubry, Octave. *The King of Rome, Napoleon II, 'L'Aiglon'* Philadelphia: J. B. Lippincott Company, 1939.

Beatty, Michael A. *The English Royal Family of America, from Jamestown to the American Revolution*. Jefferson: McFarland & Co, 2003.

Bell, Robert. *The Life of the Rt. Hon. George Canning*. London: Harper, 1955.

Bonaparte, Napoleon. *Letters and Documents of Napoleon: The Rise to Power*. Paris: Cresset Press, 1962.

Boulinier, G. En Passant par le Nord: La Dynastie des Laveran (des chirurgiens dentistes au prix Nobel de médecine). *Histoire des Sciences Médicales*. 1997; 31(2): pp.151–9.

Campbell, Thomas. *Frederick the Great: His Court and Times, Vol. 1*. London: Henry Colburn, 1842.

Campbell Orr, Clarissa. *Queenship in Europe 1660–1815: The Role of the Consort*. Cambridge: Cambridge University Press, 2004.

Carlyle, Thomas and Cromwell, Oliver (ed). *The Complete Works of Thomas Carlyle, Volume 10*. London: PF Collier, 1901.

Carrell, Jennifer Lee. *The Speckled Monster*. New York: Plume, 2004.

Childe-Pemberton, William Shakespear. *The Romance of Princess Amelia*. London: John Lane Company, 1911.

Commire, Anne and Klezmer, Deborah. *Women in World History: A Biographical Encyclopedia, Vol 17*. Waterford: Yorkin Publications, 2002.

Craig, William Marshall. *Memoir of Her Majesty Sophia Charlotte of Mecklenburg Strelitz, Queen of Great Britain*. Liverpool: Henry Fisher, 1818.

Culpeper, Nicholas. *Culpeper's English Physician*. London: The British Directory Office, 1788.

Curtiss, Mina Kirstein. *A Forgotten Empress: Anna Ivanovna and her Era, 1730–1740*. New York: Ungar, 1974.

Dixon, Simon. *Catherine the Great*. London: Profile Books, 2009.

Du Plessix Gray, Francine. *At Home with the Marquis de Sade*. London: Random House, 2013.

Edwards, Averyl. *Frederick Louis, Prince of Wales, 1701–1751*.London: Staples Press, 1947.

Fraser, Antonia. *Marie Antoinette: The Journey*. London: Phoenix, 2001.

Fraser, Flora. *Princesses: The Six Daughters of George III*. Edinburgh: A&C Black, 2012.

Fraser, Flora. *The Unruly Queen: The Life of Queen Caroline*. London: Bloomsbury Publishing, 2012.

Gill, Gillian. *We Two: Victoria and Albert: Rulers, Partners, Rivals*. New York: Ballentine Books, 2009.

Hadlow, Janice. *The Strangest Family: The Private Lives of George III, Queen Charlotte and the Hanoverians*. London: William Collins, 2014.

Hardenbroek, Gijsbert Jan van. *Gedenkschriften*. Amsterdam: J Müller, 1918.

Hardman, John. *Louis XVI: The Silent King and the Estates*. New Haven: Yale University Press, 1994.

Hatton, Ragnhild. *George I*. London: Thames and Hudson. 1978.

Hetherington Fitzgerald, Percy. *The Life of George the Fourth*. London: Tinsley Brothers, 1881.

Hibbert, Christopher. *George III: A Personal History*. London: Viking, 1998.

Hilliam, David. *Kings, Queens, Bones & Bastards: Who's Who in the English Monarchy from Egbert to Elizabeth II*. Stroud: The History Press, 2014.

Holcroft, Thomas (trans) *Posthumous Works of Frederick II, King of Prussia, Vol XIII*. London: GGJ & J Robinson, 1785.

Hunt, Margaret. *Women in Eighteenth-Century Europe*. New York: Routledge, 2014.

Imbert de Saint-Armand, Arthur Laeon & Perry, Thomas Sargeant. *The Happy Days of the Empress Marie Louise*. New York: Charles Scribner's Sons, 1898.

Inglis, Lucy. *Georgian London: Into the Streets*. London: Viking, 2013.

Iremonger, Lucille. *Love and the Princesses*. New York: Thomas Y Crowell Company, 1958.

Jerrold, Clare. *The Story of Dorothy Jordan*. London: Eveleigh Nash, 1914.

Julicher, Peter. *Renegades, Rebels and Rogues Under the Tsars*. Jefferson: McFarland & Co, 2003.

Kiste, John van der. *King George II and Queen Caroline*. Stroud: The History Press, 2013.

Kiste, John van der. *The Romanovs.* Stroud: The History Press, 2013.

Laquer, Thomas W. The Queen Caroline Affair: Politics as Art in the Reign of George IV. *The Journal of Modern History.* Vol. 54, No. 3 (Sep., 1982), pp.417–466

Lichtenau, Wilhelmine Enke. *The Confessions of the Celebrated Countess of Lichtenau.* London: JW Myers, 1799.

Lovat-Fraser, JA. *John Stuart Earl of Bute.* Cambridge: Cambridge University Press, 1912.

McCallum, Jack Edward. *Military Medicine: From Ancient Times to the 21st Century.* Santa Barbara: ABC-CLIO, 2008.

Mansel, Philip. *Louis XVIII.* Stroud: Sutton Publishing, 1999.

Marschner, Joanna. *Queen Caroline: Cultural Politics at the Early Eighteenth Century Court.* New Haven: Yale University Press, 2014.

Mary Theresa Charlotte, Duchess of Angoulême. *Royal Memoirs of the French Revolution.* London: John Murray, 1823.

Morand, Paul. *The Captive Princess: Sophia Dorothea of Celle.* Florida: American Heritage Press, 1972.

Mossiker, Frances. *The Queen's Necklace.* New York: Simon and Schuster, 1961.

Nagel, Susan. Marie-Therese, *Child of Terror: The Fate of Marie Antoinette's Daughter.* London: Bloomsbury Publishing, 2010.

Namier, Lewis. *Vanished Supremacies: Essays on European History, 1812–1918.* London: Hamish Hamilton Ltd, 1958.

Nightingale, Joseph. *Memoirs of the Last Days of Her Late Most Gracious Majesty Caroline, Queen of Great Britain, and Consort of King George the Fourth.* London: J Robins and Company, 1822.

Oulton, CW. *Authentic and Impartial Memoirs of Her Late Majesty: Charlotte Queen of Great Britain and Ireland.* London: Kinnersley, 1819.

Percy, Elizabeth. *The Diaries of a Duchess: Extracts from the Diaries of the First Duchess of Northumberland 1716–1776.* New York: George H. Doran Company, 1927.

Plowden, Alison. *Caroline and Charlotte.* Stroud: The History Press, 2011.

Powell, William. *Royal Sex: Mistresses & Lovers of the British Royal Family.* Stroud: Amberley Publishing, 2013.

Probert, Rebecca. *Marriage, Law and Practice in the Long 18th Century: A Reassessment.* Cambridge: Cambridge University Press, 2009.

Radzinsky, Edvard. *Alexander II: The Last Great Tsar.* New York: Free Press, 2006.

Rhodes, John. *The End of Plagues: The Global Battle Against Infectious Disease.* New York: Macmillan, 2013.

Richardson, Joanne. *The Disastrous Marriage.* London: Jonathan Cape, 1960.

Riedel, S. Edward Jenner and the history of smallpox and vaccination. *Proceedings.* (Baylor University Medical Center). 2005; 18(1): pp.21–25.

Robins, Jane. *The Trial of Queen Caroline.* New York: Simon & Schuster, 2006.

Rounding, Virginia. *Catherine the Great.* London: Hutchinson, 2007.

Saint Denis, Louis Etienne. *Napoleon: From the Tuileries to St. Helena*. New York: Harper & Brothers, 1922.

Scott, Walter. *The Miscellaneous Works of Sir Walter Scott: Vol IX*. Edinburgh: Adam and Charles Black, 1870.

Sebag Montefiore, Simon. *Catherine the Great and Potemkin: The Imperial Love Affair*. London: Orion, 2010.

Shawe-Taylor, Desmond and Burchard, Wolf. *The First Georgians: Art and Monarchy 1714–1760*. London: Royal Collection Trust, 2014.

Smith, EA. *George IV*. Bury St Edmunds: St Edmundsbury Press, 1999.

Smith, William James (ed.). *The Grenville Papers, Volume 4*. London: John Murray, 1853.

Smollett, Tobias and Gaspey Thomas. *The History of England: Vol III*. London: The London Printing and Publishing Company, 1800.

Tidridge, Nathan. *Prince Edward, Duke of Kent: Father of the Canadian Crown*. Toronto, Dundurn, 2013,

Tillyard, Stella. *A Royal Affair: George III and his Troublesome Siblings*. London: Vintage, 2007.

Troyat, Henri. *Catherine the Great*. New York: Dutton, 1980.

Vehse, Carl Eduard. *Memoirs of the Court of Prussia*. London: T Nelson and Sons, 1854.

Von Metternich, Klemens Wenzel Lothar, Fürst von. *Memoirs of Prince Metternich, 1773–1815*. New York: Charles Scribner's Sons, 1880.

Waldie, A. *Waldie's Select Circulating Library*. Philadelphia: Adam Waldie, 1837.

Walpole, Horace and Doran, John (ed.). *Journal of the Reign of King George the Third*. London, Richard Bentley, 1859.

Westley FC. *The Spectator, Volume 31*. London: Joseph Clayton, 1858.

Wilkins, WH. *A Queen of Tears*. London: Longmans, Green & Co, 1904.

Worsley, Lucy. *Courtiers: The Secret History of the Georgian Court*. London: Faber & Faber, 2011.

Notes

1. *London Gazette* (London, England), July 31, 1714–August 3, 1714; issue 5247, p.1. © The British Library Board.
2. *St. James's Chronicle or the British Evening Post* (London, England), May 14, 1768 – May 17, 1768; issue 1125, p.1. © The British Library Board.
3. Fraser, Flora (2005). *Princesses: The Six Daughters of George III* (1st American ed.). New York: Knopf, p.21.
4. Ibid.
5. Oulton, CW (1819). *Authentic and Impartial Memoirs of Her Late Majesty: Charlotte Queen of Great Britain and Ireland.* London: Kinnersley, p.127.
6. *General Evening Post* (London, England), June 26, 1773 – June 29, 1773; issue 6195, p.1. © The British Library Board.
7. Fraser, Antonia (2001). *Marie Antoinette: The Journey.* London: Phoenix, p.306.
8. Aubry, Octave (1939). *The King of Rome, Napoleon II, "L'Aiglon".* Philadelphia: J. B. Lippincott Company, p.256.
9. Morand, Paul (1972). *The Captive Princess: Sophia Dorothea of Celle.* Florida: American Heritage Press, p.23.
10. Craig, William Marshall (1818). *Memoir of Her Majesty Sophia Charlotte of Mecklenburg Strelitz, Queen of Great Britain.* Liverpool: Henry Fisher, p.19.
11. Smith, William James (ed.) (1853). *The Grenville Papers, Volume 4.* London: John Murray, p.276.
12. *The Parliamentary Debates: Official Reports, Volume 26* (1816). London: HM Stationery Office, p.1067.
13. Ibid., p.1068.
14. Robins, Jane (2006). *The Trial of Queen Caroline.* New York: Simon & Schuster, p.18.
15. Richardson, Joanne (1960). *The Disastrous Marriage.* London: Jonathan Cape, p.34.
16. Bell, Robert (1955). *The Life of the Rt. Hon. George Canning.* London: Harper, p.304.
17. Aspinall, Arthur (1949). *Letters of the Princess Charlotte 1811–1817.* London: Home and Van Thal, p.165.
18. Bonaparte, Napoleon (1962). *Letters and Documents of Napoleon: The Rise to Power.* Paris: Cresset Press, p.91.

19. Saint-Armand, Imbert de (1898). *The Happy Days of the Empress Marie Louise*. New York: Charles Scribner's Sons, p.86.
20. Aspinall, Arthur (ed.) (1951). *Mrs Jordan and Her Family: Being the Unpublished Correspondence of Mrs Jordan and the Duke of Clarence, Later William IV*. London: Arthur Barker, p.23.
21. *Blackwoods Edinburgh Magazine, Vol XLIII* (1838). Edinburgh: William Blackwood and Sons, p.113.
22. *Aurora and Universal Advertiser* (London, England), Friday, February 16, 1781; issue 29, p.2. © The British Library Board.
23. *Morning Herald and Daily Advertiser* (London, England), Tuesday, April 3, 1781; issue 132, p.2. © The British Library Board.
24. *True Briton* (1793) (London, England), Thursday, November 23, 1797; issue 1534, p.4. © The British Library Board.
25. Childe-Pemberton, William Shakespear (1911). *The Romance of Princess Amelia*. London: John Lane Company, p.227.
26. *The Morning Post* (London, England), Tuesday, June 24, 1806; issue 12029, p.3. © The British Library Board.
27. Ibid.
28. *Cobbett's Weekly Political Register* (London, England), Saturday, October 18, 1806; issue 16, p.1. © The British Library Board.
29. *The Morning Chronicle* (London, England), Saturday, November 11, 1820; issue 16082, pp.2–3. © The British Library Board.
30. Ibid.
31. Ibid.
32. Ibid., p.3.
33. Carlyle, Thomas and Cromwell, Oliver (ed) (1901). *The Complete Works of Thomas Carlyle, Volume 10*. London: PF Collier, p.87.
34. Smollett, Tobias and Gaspey, Thomas (1800). *The History of England: Vol III*. London: The London Printing and Publishing Company, p.694.
35. Holcroft, Thomas (trans.) (1785). *Posthumous Works of Frederick II, King of Prussia, Vol XIII*. London: GGJ & J Robinson, p26.
36. Scott, Walter (1870). *The Miscellaneous Works of Sir Walter Scott: Vol IX*. Edinburgh: Adam and Charles Black, p.88.
37. Fraser, Antonia (2001). *Marie Antoinette: The Journey*. London: Phoenix, p.526.
38. Hetherington Fitzgerald, Percy (1881). *The Life of George the Fourth*. London: Tinsley Brothers, p.909.
39. Ibid.
40. *The History of the Times: "The Thunderer" in the Making, 1785–1841* (1950), p.268.
41. *The Derby Mercury* (Derby, England), Wednesday, June 21, 1837; Issue 5476, p.3. © The British Library Board.

Index